Born in Canada, Jennifer Klinec lives in London.

'A moving meditation on love across cultures and the evocative power of food' *The Lady*

THE
TEMPORARY
BRIDE

*A Memoir of Love
and Food in Iran*

Jennifer Klinec

virago

VIRAGO

First published in Great Britain in 2014 by Virago Press
This paperback edition published in 2015 by Virago Press

1 3 5 7 9 10 8 6 4 2

A CIP catalogue record for this book
is available from the British Library.

ISBN 978-1-84408-824-9

Typeset in Bembo by M Rules
Printed and bound in Great Britain by
Clays Ltd, St Ives plc

Papers used by Virago are from well-managed forests
and other responsible sources.

MIX
Paper from
responsible sources
FSC® C104740

Virago Press
An imprint of
Little, Brown Book Group
Carmelite House
50 Victoria Embankment
London EC4Y 0DZ

An Hachette UK Company
www.hachette.co.uk

www.virago.co.uk

For my mother. For Vahid

Prologue

We have begun what has grown into a daily ritual. It starts with me taking my morning's thrill-seeking taxi ride through the crowded streets of Yazd, to her apartment complex on the edge of the city. Normally each morning, I ask the driver to stop on the way to buy flowers and he frets impatiently as I pick through the wilted irises and tulips that have somehow found their way to this place in the desert. But this morning's driver makes me uncomfortable, so I don't ask him to stop.

Older than the other taxi drivers I've had, he isn't sporting the latest gelled-up, parrot hairstyle. No sun-bleached, hand-lettered taxi sign is strapped onto the roof of his car. Despite the ninety-degree weather he is wearing a jacket over a thick, coarse-wool sweater. His car smells faintly of rosewater and tobacco.

As he drives he clacks a string of wooden prayer beads

loudly between his fingers. The dashboard is taped up with worn prints of bearded prophets in fading shades of green. He is the kind of devout, unsmiling man I can still feel intimidated by.

He is silent during the twenty-minute journey from where he picked me up, honking and swerving his battered Paykan to where I'd stood at the curb. This is likely a second job, carried out for a few hours each morning, the consequence of rising inflation and three currency devaluations in the last year alone.

I reach down to fidget with the length of rust-coloured cotton resting in my lap from the scarf that loosely circles my head. A new habit picked up quickly. A green-handled screwdriver jammed into the gap next to my window rattles as we turn down the dusty, wide road lined with sand-coloured brick buildings where Vahid lives with his parents. I hand over the equivalent of ten dollars, more than double what the trip should cost, and know enough not to wait for change.

In the three days that I have been coming here the guards have quickly learned my face. They look up from their newspapers to wave me through the entrance and up the stairs.

Vahid's mother wears black every day. I want to greet her with a hug but it's still too soon. She keeps her scarf on each time I come and lowers her head when I try to take photographs. Over cups of cinnamon tea we thumb through our combined collection of cookbooks to plan the day's menu: chicken in pomegranate and walnut sauce or a fish stew fragrant with fenugreek and tamarind, the latter a speciality of her native Khuzestan.

We sit on the floor with a silver tray between us, sorting through mountains of fresh mint, basil and parsley. I rip away roots knotted with sand and tiny pebbles, and slosh the leaves through a bucket of salt water. She tears the skins from a pile of onions and slices them in her hand. Her small knife strikes against her palm and neat, tidy crescents fall away into a plastic bowl. She measures rice, dipping a chipped cup rimmed with gold and patterned with roses that lives inside the bag for exactly this purpose. Four cups full instead of three, because I am still considered a guest and it would be a great shame if I were not given extra when the meal is served.

I can sense by the way she smiles at me and her deep sighs of '*akheish*' that I am tipping the balance in this house. I imagine she's been missing the presence of her only female child. Vahid's sister lives near the Iraqi border, twenty-six hours away by bus. She hums while we work, a humming that sounds too powerful for her slight build, a humming that sounds neither calming nor cheery. Instead, it wafts around me in a way that keeps me aware of her presence, a centre of gravity in the kitchen we share.

Neither Vahid nor his father says much to her during our long mornings cooking together. Instead they attempt rudimentary repairs. The enormous cooler is removed from where it hangs suspended from the ceiling. They pry the filters loose with screwdrivers and take them to the balcony to bang them free of dust. Their tasks are social, involving long consultations with neighbours and the seeking of advice. Hers is solitary, the work of the sole woman of the house. They enter the kitchen only to reach around her to steal a peeled carrot from a bowl or a stray piece of cauliflower. Otherwise I see them only at mealtimes when they return from outdoors or rise from their places on the scarlet and navy carpet to throw open the door to the daily tide of relatives who wash in at lunchtime.

Each day, as the house fills with the aroma of saffron, pomegranate syrup or onions fried in butter, our work is not unlike that of some ancient royal court. We decorate each dish with swirls of cream and stripes of chopped herbs. We snap the *sofreh* tablecloth sharply in the air. Without speaking, we glide our palms over it in a co-ordinated motion, smoothing any creases from its gold-threaded pattern after laying it on the floor. We cover it with platters of rice flecked with barberries, bowls of fragrant stews and little jars of the home-made pickles labelled in her hand. The men are quick to sit, eating everything almost without speaking, their eyes glued to the television. As their plates empty they are automatically refilled by their wives. Scraps of fire-singed bread are set before them; the handle of the *doogh* pitcher, the drinking yoghurt Vahid's mother leaves on the window ledge each night to ferment and turn fizzy, is turned towards them for their easy reach. In this house life quietly arranges itself around the men who watch CNN and the BBC.

I half listen but I am not so interested. The reporter is talking about the upcoming elections. Ahmadinejad is making a speech. As the men struggle to understand the English voiceover they attempt loud interpretations – a commentary of pointing and shouting, with mouths half full of the food we have cooked. No one thinks to ask me.

Vahid's father is always the loudest. 'Down, down America.'

Tea follows lunch. The pots and dishes are gathered up and brought to the kitchen. Leftovers are scraped into empty yoghurt containers to be reheated for dinner, and plates and cutlery are piled into the sink. I roll up my sleeves to wash the dishes but Vahid's mother shoos me away. She gestures that I should sit instead with the men; a treat for me. I glance at Vahid's father and uncles who remain sitting on the floor, dislodging particles from their teeth with wooden toothpicks. I shuffle across the room towards an aunt instead. She and I take turns cutting a pile of oval *toftoon* bread with scissors, stacking the pieces in quarters and wrapping them in cloth for the evening's meal. When we finish I feel her press a ring into my hand. It is heavy and silver with a gaudy red stone. I smile as I try it on, pressing my fingers together to keep it from sliding off.

'She is very proud to give you that ring which she bought in Mecca,' says Vahid. 'You are the first foreigner she has ever met so she wants you to have it. But don't worry,' he adds, 'I know you think it's ugly so you don't have to wear it.'

The latch on the hall closet makes a tinny clink when opened, signifying the start of the afternoon naps. We reach for the pillows stashed inside and the woollen blankets safety-pinned with thin, cotton coverings. The women retire to one room while the men sleep in another. As I tiptoe cautiously around the moms and aunties who have already settled themselves into tidy rows on the floor, there is a giddy atmosphere of freedom that comes from separation from men. It is only my third or fourth day of coming here but already I have a usual spot, in the corner underneath the thick yellow curtains that shield us from view.

I hear coughs and faint snoring from the living room, and catch glimpses of Vahid's father and uncles, wrapped loosely in sheets. They have stripped down to the grey cotton long underwear they wear under their trousers. Elasticated, cuffed ankles jut out in all directions. The whispered prayers of the women around me soften into quiet breathing. I am amazed once more by the ease with which they fall asleep with me, still a stranger, among them.

Though the intimacy of the moment prevents me from sleeping, I feel pleased to have earned my place on their floor.

Suddenly, by accident, I have found myself pulled – even accepted – into the inner circle of an Iranian household. As a warm feeling of affection washes over me, I close my eyes and fall asleep.

Chapter One

Growing up, my memories of the kitchen were of being chased out of it by my mother. Frazzled from a long day at work but committed to putting something home-made on our dinner table, she wanted no obstacles, no potential spillages, and certainly none of our eager curiosity in the way as she rushed to peel potatoes or slice raw onions into a cucumber salad. The consequence of her efficiency was that I didn't learn to cook a thing from my mother. Not a thing.

I was born in south-western Ontario to immigrant parents. The rural county road where we lived was little more than a gravel track and a kind of wild, pioneer lifestyle was in force. People burned their own garbage and showered in sulphur-smelling water pumped up from wells. They shot raccoons and occasionally each other's barn cats with hunting rifles. A big yellow bus collected my sister and me at the end of our driveway each morning for the

1

hour-long journey to school. It didn't take long to figure out that we were a little weirder than the Anglo-Saxon kids in our neighbourhood. Carcasses of lambs or pigs were roasted over a spit on our front lawn. Thermoses of stewed giblets and cabbage were put into our lunch boxes. My mom's sour-cherry strudel stood out at bake sales against the towering jello moulds and Rice Krispie squares. Boneless, skinless chicken breasts weren't part of our food vocabulary. In spite of my banishment, I was as voracious and eager a child as could be. My mother's forbidden kitchen with its meaty, paprika-dense scent captured my imagination and I devoured every drop of her sour-cream-thickened stews, her fluffy semolina dumplings and the vinegary cabbage salads she crushed between her fingers.

Our house was strict and mealtimes were sacred. Unlike my classmates who ate dinner at five-thirty from plates in their laps in their basement rec rooms or in front of the TV, we rarely ate before eight o'clock and always at the table. My mother, who frequently went back and forth to fetch cold beers for my father, sat nearest the kitchen. His place close to the window was marked by a dish of olives and an empty plate for bones. Bones of all shapes were a revered item in our house and we learned early to twist chicken wings in our mouths to snap them in two and scrape our teeth against pork ribs to seek out the satisfying tear of their tasty, paper-thin membranes.

My parents were part of a generation of strivers for whom money and gain meant everything. My father had arrived in Toronto in the late 1960s with twenty-one dollars in his pocket and not a word of English. He considered his thick Hungarian accent to be his biggest curse and vowed that his own children would speak perfectly. He kept us away from the groups of other Eastern Europeans who met frequently in halls and church basements to socialise and pine for 'the old country'. Instead he worked day and night shifts as an electrician, said yes to anything else that came up in between and built a New World cocoon around all of us. He never returned to the flatlands of northern Serbia where he was raised, not even when his father was dying of lung cancer.

My mother came to Canada on a boat with my grandmother when she was five, sailing from the Yugoslavian port of Rijeka to Montreal. My grandmother had become pregnant with her just after getting married. My mother remembers little of the journey to Canada, only that she was sick most of the way. My grandfather, like many of his generation, was fiercely patriotic and couldn't bear to see Croatia fall under the influence of communism. While my grandmother was pregnant, he went off to join one of Yugoslavia's many wars, then emigrated via Austria to Canada, leaving them behind. My mother was born on a bed of straw in a barn that had been cleared of livestock. For five years they ate little but dried bread moistened with salted water or bean broth. Eventually my grandfather was pressured to apply for visas for them and to send money for their boat passage. My grandparents slept in separate bedrooms for as long as I can remember.

My grandmother, Baba Stanešič, learned her English mainly from watching television, which gave her an abrupt, stilted way of speaking. Combined with her humourless face and the violence of her gestures, she could scatter neighbourhood children off her driveway in a matter of seconds. My grandmother was nothing like the *mémés* and *nanas* of my school friends who were all cuddles, home-baked shortbread and blind, unconditional love. Our *baba* preferred to fill our heads with talk of death, superstition and the curses of menopause. Her walls were hung with paintings of Jesus, and her drawers were filled with Kotex. Come winter or summer, she wore thick woollen tights.

When we took her to lunch at one of the nondescript chain restaurants that filled our city, she dismissed our offers to visit the salad bar, demanding loudly that she wanted to eat meat. She wore saggy purple sweat pants under a long, navy trenchcoat every day except Sundays, when she wore every stick of jewellery she owned to church. Bursting with her crocheted doilies, Croatian flags, photographs of Tito and religious icons, her house had an ornate, museum-like quality, full of things I was to look at but never touch. The only times I felt close to her were on the occasions we went there for lunch, when she cooked the food of a peasant childhood. Her golden chicken broth glistened with pools of fat and swam with tiny home-made egg noodles and her salty cabbage rolls were stewed with leather-like hunks of smoked sausage. I watched in awe as she grated cabbages on a wooden mandoline, her broad shoulders and man-like arms packing them with salt into glass jars, storing them to ferment in her eerie, spiderless cellar with walls so red my sister used to tell me they had been painted with pig's blood. Her desserts were neither light nor colourful but dense, dark and unflashy, *bundt* sponges infused with coffee or chocolate, cakes made with cornmeal and pulverised walnuts, hazelnut crescents rolled thickly in powdered sugar.

When my sister and I were ten and eleven, on the brink of becoming teenagers, our grandmother began a campaign of counsel and advice about men – how to catch them, how to keep them, and how she believed we should make them happy. She criticised our physical appearance – the cut-off jeans and plastic flip-flops we wore, and the combs we quickly dragged through our hair – insisting that 'If you want to get married, you need to wear tight black dresses and lots of make-up!' Once we hit menstruating age, she chased us away from stone fireplace hearths and boulders in the garden, cold surfaces she believed would affect our ability to have children if sat upon, and she chastised me for my long, thrillingly fast bicycle rides, claiming they threatened my virginity. She told us that, once we were married, we had a duty to keep our houses clean and our fridges well stocked or our husbands were entitled to beat us until we were shades of blue and purple.

When my parents met I imagine they were perfect for each other. My mother, who had remained an only child, was then fifteen. Her childhood was primarily a solitary one and although she'd become an attractive teenager, she was shy and inexperienced. My father was twenty-one and just beginning to feel the pangs of exile. He drank, smoked, had long sideburns and was confidently handsome. My mother tells me he thought of himself as a bit of a ladies' man. Arriving in Canada to find that his electrician's qualifications meant nothing was hard on him. For two years he resorted to driving a taxi at night while he studied English and prepared to qualify for a Canadian certification. His new life was unexpectedly lonely. No one could pronounce or spell his name correctly. No one appreciated his dry sense of humour. One day when he was working on a construction site, he told the foreman's assistant that his name was 'MacKlinec' after all the Scotsmen he'd encountered, and she punched the lettering into a piece of red adhesive tape that he wore on the front of his hard hat.

My mother gave my father somewhere to nest and put down roots. My father gave my mother the affection and sense of belonging she craved. They had in common both a language (Serbo-Croatian) and a strong urge to escape their pasts. After a three-year courtship which saw my father driving three hours each weekend to see her, sleeping on the couch in my grandparents' basement, they married, just weeks after my mother finished high school. My sister was born almost immediately and I came along thirteen months later. My parents became not just husband and wife but a team, in love with each other and with who they felt they could be. Their excesses of pride and showy, physical displays of affection often drove my sister and me to leave the room from an early age, feeling that we were trespassing.

By the time I was eight years old my parents had begun to realise their ambitions and in the process lost their taste for hands-on parenting. Though their love for us was never in question, it changed into a kind of benevolent neglect. They ran their automotive manufacturing business while we became feral, wealthy children. Our bedrooms were full of the latest gadgets – VCRs and Sony Walkmans – but our birthdays went unnoticed and our clothes unwashed. We were handed keys to the house on chains and told to let ourselves in after school. My mother woke us up in the morning with a telephone call.

We took advantage of our situation by playing hookey from our strict French-Catholic primary school. I'd inform the school secretary of our absence in my best nine-year-old adult voice and on cue my sister would produce a breakfast of grape ice cream and microwave popcorn. We'd spend the day playing Monopoly and watching terrifying reruns of *Dark Shadows*, a far more appealing alternative to spending it under the watchful eyes of the nuns at the École St Joseph.

Hemmed in by my parents' hunger for money and their yearning to compensate for childhoods of eating maize and cabbage while owning nothing, we began eating sirloin steak three times a week. The other nights we ordered in pizza or picked up KFC. Our luscious, peasant evening meals began to disappear. My sister, who had loathed our family traditions, was delighted but I was devastated. Our dinner table became solemn and lifeless, my parents talking car parts and volumes and shipments, while my sister and I, as silent as ghosts, ate quickly and vanished into our bedrooms.

Our humble family ceremonies – eating salamis hung in the woodshed by my father; roasting slabs of bacon on sticks over the coals of the fireplace; cooking goulash in summer in a rusty pot hanging from a chain – became a distant memory. I longed for the times when we'd sit, my mother, father, sister and me, on cheap folding chairs in the garden, my father's gypsy music on the portable cassette player, my mother's chickens scratching for worms on the lawn. Saying little, we weren't an emotional family, we ate, complimented the meal, the warm evening, the good fortune of owning land and the property around us.

By the age of ten I possessed a sense of independence that astonished my friends' mothers. It was marked officially if unintentionally by silver when my mother dropped me off at school late from the dentist. Sliding my tongue tentatively over a mouthful of new metal fillings, I raced around the sharp contours of her Lincoln Continental, which were already crusted over with early summer flies. Her outstretched hand held a brown lunch bag of veal skewers breaded in crushed Ritz crackers. Her foot was already on the gas as she placed a warm, garlicky kiss on my forehead and I had to holler to remind her that I needed a note for my teacher to explain my lateness. She rummaged through her purse for a pen. 'Can't you just write the note yourself?' she sighed. I nodded, eager as always to please her, yet stunned to be commissioned with an act of forgery. My mother handed me the pen, along with an empty McDonald's French-fries packet she'd found on the floor of the back seat, and sped off to work.

From that point on, I faithfully recreated my mother's unkempt script, effectively becoming my own signatory and acting guardian. I signed my report cards and letters of consent, even my registration for high school. Every August I was deposited at the mall with several hundred dollars in cash and told to buy my clothes for the new school year. With any other child it would have been a recipe for disaster but there was never any fear I would return home with short skirts or a punk wardrobe. I viewed this freedom and autonomy as something precious, something to safeguard, giving my parents the low-maintenance child they needed most.

Adults began to speak to me like an adult, mistaking me for a university student by the time I was thirteen. Instead of seeking to prolong my youth my parents continued to be exasperated by it, by the balancing act of keeping me occupied. Their pragmatism permitted me to assume more responsibility for myself, making choices about how I spent my summer holidays. I enrolled myself in swimming and gymnastics lessons, subsisted on chicken sandwiches and Fudgesicles at the local Y cafeteria. I travelled back and forth by taxi, paying for it all with money left in a special drawer in the hallway. At the end of each day my mother expressed little interest in my progress in front crawl or the parallel bars, insisting instead on an inventory of what I'd eaten that day, seeking peace of mind that my stomach hadn't gone empty.

Little by little I began to outgrow my parents. I decided if I was to be lonely under their roof, better still to be truly alone. For spring break, while my friends went off in vans with their families to Disneyland or Myrtle Beach, I asked my mother to drop me off at our summer cottage. She waded through the snow with me to ensure I could turn the key in the door, leaving me with enough groceries to last me the week. She knew I wouldn't be scared, didn't even need to ask me. By then, she trusted I knew what I was doing. I built fires, went for long snowy walks, past all the other cottages that stood vacant. The snow on their porches was uncleared, long, pointed icicles hanging from their eaves. I vacuumed, mopped and scrubbed the bathtub, savouring the responsibilities of looking after myself. I chose to sleep in my creaky wooden bed in the smallest room, even though my parents' double bed was available. For ten kilometres in any direction I was the only living person and I learned I could happily go for days without talking to another person.

Soon I thought nothing of covering great distances alone, craving the departure, the sense of breaking away. At sixteen, I was desperate to taste life outside of our industrial Ontario city, dominated by the smokestacks of Chrysler, Ford and General Motors. Financed by my father and mother, and fuelled by my own sheer nerve, I enrolled myself in a Swiss boarding school. In the last, final stages in the car to the airport I itched to leave as soon as possible, discouraging my parents from seeing me to the gate. It meant everything to walk those last few hundred yards unaccompanied. As I turned a corner, leaving them behind, I felt myself cry out in relief. For the first time in my life I felt truly free.

At school I made friends, staying up past curfew to gossip with my two roommates, sharing tables in the dining hall and eating lunch off trays, but I continued to crave solitude and escape. I telephoned my mother and asked her to lie about a family relative in Switzerland so I could spend American Thanksgiving alone. I booked myself a couchette to Vienna while my classmates went in small groups to Paris and Florence. With two months of German lessons, I arrived at the Westbahnhof, angering taxi drivers who didn't know the address of the tiny pension I'd written down on a piece of paper. Exasperated, they drove in circles, searching for Kirchengasse, frustrated by my pronunciation, causing me nearly to break down in tears. It reduced me to wondering what had possessed me to undertake such a thing alone, refusing to go out again that night, sitting on my narrow bed, listening to the unfamiliar sound of trams rolling past. Yet by the next morning the city felt less unfriendly, the streets more forgiving. I began to enjoy the first moments of walking through a new place, having to decipher how things worked: the structure and layout of the streets, the way to order a coffee.

For Easter and summer breaks I sought places that felt increasingly uncomfortable, looking to push myself further into unfamiliar territories. I went alone to Corsica, Iceland and Bosnia, returning each time to boarding school feeling capable and alive. Among my classmates, who whispered and flashed me looks of disdain, I developed a reputation for being aloof, but younger teachers admired my wilfulness and sense of calm, inviting me for coffee and glasses of wine, or to share grown-up dinners of Brie and pâté in the small apartments they lived in off campus.

Going away alone let me retreat into something innocent and unsure – a kind of rebellion, after having become an adult so early. I learned to identify the environments I preferred: lunchrooms with oppressive wooden furniture decorated in plastic tablecloths; corner tobacconists offering muddy espressos and salami and raw-onion sandwiches; workers' canteens where the cutlery on each table stood in a single glass. Eventually I grew confident enough to enter even all-male taverns, where red-faced patrons often ate standing up at counters, smoking. I rented cheap rooms in the homes of pensioners reached by creaky tram carriages, snacking on meat fried on street corners in front of graffiti-covered apartment blocks.

I started to change how I dressed, aspiring to look less North American. I gave away my frayed jeans and moccasins, my clothes covered with logos bought at the mall. Instead I chose muted colours, knee-length skirts with boots; I wore my hair simply – tied back or cut into a bob. People asked if I was Scandinavian or addressed me in French, presuming less and less that I was a foreigner or a tourist. I enjoyed sitting alone in railway carriages, relishing my first taste of alcohol in bars, feeling mysterious and flattered when men began to stare at me for the first time. I learned I had a knack for languages, overcoming any shyness, feeling resourceful enough to speak broken Italian in Romania or to piece together scraps of Portuguese. I was soon able to decipher signs written in Cyrillic and understand everything written on packets in Dutch.

It was a sense of motion that thrilled me, that sustained my sense of progress and reminded me I had come a long way from home. The ultimate satisfaction came in airports, seeing my name printed on boarding passes, handling the increasingly worn pages of my passport as if I'd always been destined for travel. Rarely did I stuff my documents back in my pocket without pausing to contemplate my strange, distorted, Hungarian name. A name that in principle should never have strayed from the flatland villages my parents came from, that was never intended to travel further away than thirty kilometres by train.

After a year of boarding school, considering myself too old for its rules and restrictions, I transferred to a school in Dublin. I was ready to live on my own and had decided that it would be easier to do so for the first time in an English-speaking country. I rented a cheap attic apartment in a Georgian terrace on the south side of the city, overlooking Dublin Bay, and there I found the love of my life: I began to teach myself to cook.

As a seventeen-year-old living alone, away from her parents – going to a school full of O'Connells and Donnellys – I was an anomaly, probably even illegal, but thanks to a greediness for my school fees we pretended not to notice. I studied Joyce, Yeats, calculus and Russian against a backdrop of whispered theories about my perceived orphanhood. I compensated for any loneliness by attempting meals from my first cookbook, a hardcover edition called *Foods of the World* I'd pulled from a two-pound bargain bin during a trip to London.

I became engrossed in its descriptions of foods I'd never heard of or tasted: Iraqi polo, Szechuan hot-pot, fish roasted in banana leaves. In my primitive kitchen with its scratched linoleum floor and two-ring electric stove, I made Irish approximations of exotic recipes, using whatever ingredients I could lay my hands on. I shelled prawns and boiled couscous, chopped coriander and aubergines with my Swiss army knife. I became fond of pasta with garlic, chilli and olive oil, and Moroccan lamb and chickpea stew. By the end of the school year I'd both established my culinary foothold and lost my virginity; the latter with one of my classmates, made possible by a visit to the Well Woman Clinic and its doctor who shoved me back into the street with a paper bag of illegal (in Ireland) birth control pills.

During this time my mother had imagined I'd subsisted on spaghetti and tuna fish. When I returned to Canada at the end of the year, she was shocked to see my tall, skinny frame had gained two kilos. Instead of being shunted out of the kitchen, I now took my rightful place beside her, forming a partnership as tender and sturdy as the fingerprints we pressed into the chestnut-flour dumplings that we scattered on soft tea towels. She taught me my favourite childhood recipes – crisp, pencil-thin schnitzel, fat egg noodles with blackened fried onions, a savoury summer concoction of beans in paprika and sour cream that as children we'd dubbed 'bean mush' – and in return I taught her gazpacho, seared tuna and spinach with chillies and mustard seeds. Through our collaboration we remedied our ill-defined mother–daughter relationship and declared culinary war on my father who was otherwise determined to eat steak at least four times a week. Sometimes, perhaps regretful that I had once been chased away from the space I now inhabited with such confidence, my mother would smile wistfully and touch my cheek with her floury, sweet-smelling hands. When I left for school we spoke on the phone almost daily and our first question to each other was always the same: 'What are you having for dinner tonight?'

Throughout university in Montreal I continued to cook, discovering markets, fishmongers and the fascinating, musty shops of Chinatown. Braving the long six-month winters and regular temperatures of minus thirty-five degrees, I trudged through the snow to buy still-warm baguettes and to shop for defiantly unpasteurised *fromage* made by rogue Québécois farmers. My surrogate kitchen parents – Alice Waters, Hugh Carpenter and Biba Caggiano – nudged me into the culinary wilderness of raw fish, fennel, mussels and lemongrass, and in between lectures I made Shanghai noodles with black beans and clams, or fresh ravioli stuffed with pumpkin.

My moving to Britain was sudden and unexpected. I'd been out walking my dog when a man visiting from New Zealand asked me for directions. He was wearing flip-flops even though it was nearly November. We had a cup of coffee that lasted three days. Four months later we were on a plane to Glasgow with Commonwealth work visas stamped in our passports. My father was furious. He hadn't immigrated to the New World, he insisted, only for his children to turn round and go back to the old one. His expectation was that I might find a job in Chicago or eventually take over the family factory. My romance fizzled out after six months, but I chose to stay on in the UK, landing my first real job, in a large investment bank in London.

At first, I'd marvelled at my new sense of importance. I had a desk. A digital phone. Not one, but three flat-screen monitors. The restrooms sparkled with marble and granite, and the walls of the meeting rooms were hung with art that cost more than the tiny Chelsea apartment I rented by the week. Corporate life brought me financial independence beyond my wildest dreams. I took elaborate holidays, I spent a fortune on clothes. I bought an apartment in an old shoe factory, relieving it of its rusting fixtures, adding glass and stainless steel. By day I rustled paper and helped the rich get richer, and by night I retreated, barefoot, into my new, perfect kitchen, cooking quasi-peasant food and feeling grateful for my luck.

Morning in, morning out, the months became years. As I found myself washed across marble foyers on a sea of polished shoes and grey overcoats, I started to itch with unease, even boredom. I craved an honest pride I rarely felt in banks where I was too straight, too reared on old-fashioned honour to thrive. I cringed at the sameness of it all; the people who had groomed themselves, gone to the right schools, mouthed the right phrases in their interviews, only to spend the next thirty years doing the minimum required to stay afloat. It was a lost, meaningless, immeasurable kind of work. Every morning I steeled myself, I dressed and combed my hair, and walked through the revolving doors into a living PR campaign. I slowly began to hate what I did. One of the best things about my adopted city was the ease of leaving it – London was the hub of the universe and there was nowhere you couldn't fly to. I sought fulfilment through the airways.

At first it was once or twice a month, and the occasional three-day weekend. Soon I was travelling five weekends out of every six and the trips became further and more severe. A 17.38 flight on Friday night would have me eating tripe in Naples by 9 p.m. The first ferry of the day back from an island in Sweden would allow time for a breakfast of crayfish and an icy swim on the way to catch my plane. Polish agritourism farms, Swiss 'sleep on straw' alpine barns, a backstreet apartment in a grubby quarter of Lisbon: all became second, weekend homes. Come Monday morning, I reported to my desk straight from the airport with my hair still damp with foreign water and my shoes packed with sand and clay. I became proficient in commuting from the most authentic, distant places I could get to and an expert in living for the promise of the weekend.

I went home to Canada to visit my parents. I saw how, in the years since I'd moved to Britain, a huge gulf had grown between us. I was salaried, desk-bound and lax while they toiled in their factory, stacking parts, pouring chemicals and overseeing two long, exhausting shifts per day. My mother's hands were cracked and raw while mine were smooth and rosy. I felt shamefully reminded of the ease and meaninglessness of my life, and humbled by the pride and austerity of theirs. After five days, I landed back at Heathrow with a plan. The next day, I quit my job. A week later the carpenters arrived. They built a large oak table that seated twelve and plumbed in an industrial dishwasher. Six weeks later I had my first class. My new life, my new business, 'Eat Drink Talk', was born.

Four months later I flew home again to see my mother. It was a week before Christmas and I'd been working flat out for months: sixty-hour weeks, long days on my feet, the lugging home of heavy groceries from the market. Our first evening together, we stayed up late and sat in the kitchen. She warmed up a soup of chicken and dumplings. Rubbing my eyes that were still dry from the flight, I felt my mom reach for one of my hands, tracing it with her fingers. It was chapped and sore from hours spent scrubbing pots and pans, and wiping surfaces with rags soaked in bleach. Studying it carefully, she looked back at me and I saw tears in her eyes.

'Jen,' she said tenderly, raising my hand and kissing it. 'You have labourer's hands. Just like your father and me.'

Chapter Two

The digital clock on the front of the oven shows almost midnight when I sit on the wide, short step that leads to the kitchen. It's the usual place that I mop myself to, while I wait for the floors to dry. The scent of orange-oil soap, one capful per bucket, has come to signify the end of the day.

Flicking a worn, felt house slipper off one foot with the toe of the other, I lean back against the wall. I smell like onions and black pepper. It has worked its way into the weave of my clothes and the roots of my hair. Whether the class has Oaxacan moles in it, or a whole Vietnamese-style snapper, it's guaranteed I'll walk away reeking of alliums and spice.

I rummage through the left-behind bottles, pouring the last of some red wine into the only clean glass I can find. The large metal windows – remnants of my home's previous life as a shoe factory, along with its concrete pillars and tall, bare ceilings – are opened wide and the cool spring air begins to mix with the smells of the hot kitchen. I untie the strings of the blue and brown apron printed with a fading pattern of dancing Victorian ladies and crumple it into a ball.

When I sense the floor is dry enough to move, I walk to the bathroom to add it, one final garment, to the washing machine. My lips are red and dry from not drinking enough water and my hair is pulled back into a ponytail, fixed with a black rubber band that has long lost its shape. My fingertips are stained yellow with turmeric and the polish on my toenails has worn away to misshapen dots. Three years in to this strange, wonderful new life and I look more like I did when I was a student. The same carelessness with my appearance. The same faded T-shirts and denim skirts, Birkenstocks and hooded jackets. My face is perhaps my one saving grace. Free of make-up, it has a kind of flushed, rosy glow I've always been proud of, one that leads most people to mistake me for younger than I am.

My home is over twelve hundred square feet, but for now I live out of just a small corner, in the bedroom into which I have pushed most of my belongings. My living room is strung with damp tablecloths and linen napkins hang over the kitchen stools to dry. A further load of aprons and dishcloths churns in the washing machine with a cupful of baking soda, added to remove the stains of red wine and smoked paprika. Often I fall asleep before the load has finished, still wearing my clothes and slippers, cradling a half-written shopping list, curled into a ball. My apartment is no longer my own, but shared with sixty people a week. They come here, in groups of twelve, and I teach them to cook.

There is no sign, no advertising, just a doorbell on the side of my orange brick building. When they come, my guests step into the old freight elevator that takes them up to the first floor. They are a potluck of people – strangers, often both to me and to each other – and most are young, in their twenties and thirties. Usually they like the idea of learning to cook in such an unlikely, industrial setting ('It's so underground! It could be New York!') but others are more wary. ('Do people live here?') My smile is genuine when they arrive and I take their wine bottles, putting them in the fridge, in exchange for the cocktails I have made, having juiced pink grapefruits and pomegranates by hand, and crushed fistfuls of mint and ginger with honey in the final moments before the doorbell rings.

At first I was apprehensive about what the neighbours would think and tried to keep the fact that I had turned my apartment into a makeshift cooking school quiet. It drove me to theft, stealing magazines containing reviews of my classes from their mailboxes, but they seem to tolerate me, or at least, this being Britain, they lack the courage to tell me they disapprove of the strangers who come and go.

In any case, it feels almost wrong to call them classes.

Nightly we gather around my long, wooden table, perfect for rolling dough or hand-stretching filo pastry, using coconut scrapers and dim sum rolling pins. We taste 'crazy honey' from Turkey and tongue-numbing Szechuan peppercorns from China. We crimp dumplings between our fingers and mix pickled tea leaves with roast peanuts and lime juice in tiny, lacquer Burmese bowls. Depending on the evening the table is laden with bamboo baskets and cleavers or metal rasps and paring knives; perhaps tiny Arab wooden presses for shaping the cookies we'll make with ground almonds and dates. One day is Turkish or Modern British Cooking, the next may be a Malaysian or Cambodian class. My pantry is full to bursting with the tools I pull down for an evening and carefully stack away again: a copper *ibrik* for Turkish coffee along with a dozen tiny, enamelled cups and saucers; Vietnamese mandolines for slicing green papaya and star fruit; a tortilla press for flattening balls of *masa*. I have not one but five mortars and pestles, made of granite, brass and volcanic rock.

Every morning, for three hours I shop for my classes, seeking the best and freshest ingredients I can find. The radish leaves we will crush with roasted pumpkin seeds, green chillies and *tomatillos*. The betel leaves we will wrap around minced chicken with toasted rice and Asian herbs. The fresh turmeric we will simmer in coconut milk, adding lobster, curry leaves and tamarind. Small cardboard boxes of tiny, folded quails. Round silver cans of walnut oil. Thick glass jars of crème fraîche. Fermenting and mixing. Straining and infusing. I spend hours trying to make each class perfect.

I seem to have become something of an 'it girl', which surprises me. PR firms and ad agencies book their Christmas parties here. Wine companies enquire about sherry tastings and champagne-pairing evenings. I write a column for a style magazine with recipes and photographs. It is strange for me to see my words printed alongside features on designer clothes or boutique hotels in Paris. I earn roughly half of what I used to and haven't bought a new dress in over a year. I get my hair cut every four months instead of two, and the T-shirts and jeans I live in are starting to get holes in them. There is nothing breezy or effortless about what I do but I have never, for a second, looked back.

My first meal of the day often comes at 10 p.m. My assistant Katrina and I reach for my cheap Chinese plastic bowls, the ones with red, faded dragon motifs we often eat from when all the good plates are gone, and fill them with the remaining scraps of the evening's food. Sometimes we are lucky and can feast on crab claws or the tail end of a fish; the morsels that are too messy, too full of bones for delicate English palates. More often than not, there is barely enough food for one so I pretend not to be hungry, nudging the leftovers towards Katrina and secretly making a bowl of steamed rice scattered with a few roasted peanuts after she has gone.

In the three years that we have been working together, we have seen a pattern develop. Our favourite classes are those made up of voracious people who love to eat: the Italians who push past us for the emptied pots on the stove and scrape the bottoms with hunks of bread; the skinny East End girls who loosen the belts on their black, clingy jeans as they slurp third helpings of coconut-milk soup and long-simmered curry; and the timid Japanese couples who make easy work of dark chocolate cakes that spill with warm, salted caramel. We read their appreciation not in words but in brusque table manners and devastation, the stacks of empty bowls and plates, napkins stained with oils and sauces, £150 of ingredients chopped, cooked and consumed in just under three hours.

The worst classes, the ones we dread, can usually be predicted by a glance at the class list. On unlucky nights it reads like the honour roll of some leafy private school. The tidy, pronounceable English names of people who will travel from London's tree-lined, Georgian-terraced postcodes to spend the evening with us which often fill us with a sense of despair.

These are names that struggle with chopsticks, lose patience with rolling pins and eat flatbreads with a knife and fork. Reared on a diet of boiled vegetables and lamb with mint sauce, with pasty faces and lips that screw up at the scent of fish sauce or the sour taste of tamarind, these names are often bundled with smugness on coming to see what 'this cooking lark' is all about. Our ingredients – meat streaked with fat and cartilage, fish with the heads still on, bundles of herbs bound up with twine – and our spice-roasted, wok-seared, street-food recipes are usually lost on them. They prefer delicate fillets and white wine sauces. When they go, taking their awkward silences with them but leaving behind their recipe binders, they are also the most generous. With these names the leftovers are always plentiful.

My classes are uncompromising and authentic, probably too much so. I know some people want a list of pastes and instant doughs, cheats from the supermarket, but I continue to be stubborn. Most of the time, the people who come seem to like what I do. Their appetite seems to be not just for the food we cook, but the stories I tell and the world I inhabit: the woman in Chinatown who sells me tiny swimmer crabs out of a laundry hamper; the Scottish scallop divers who wrap langoustines in copies of the *Highland Times* newspapers and send them to me on the sleeper train; the trips abroad I take to learn new recipes, staying away for weeks at a time.

The only glitch in this new life is that it can still break my heart a little; I care so much. When someone brushes past me and eyeballs the setting I've meticulously planned, or gives a cold, thin-lipped smile upon finding that there are no chef hats or thermometer-controlled water baths, I feel awkward in my plain apron and bare feet, but I am learning to be stoic. I am fighting for this way of life, which still feels new yet has subsumed everything – my home, my energy, my every waking hour. Day in day out – the scent of orange oil, dregs of red wine and the scent of onion and black pepper deep in my skin.

The washing machine is still going when the doorbell rings. It is unusual for him to come on a weekday; we usually see each other only on weekends and even that is rare. Sometimes we won't speak for months. The prompts and invitations are always by text message, always out of the blue and rarely, if ever, refused.

I take his coat and hang it up beside mine, along with the woollen scarf he wears looped around his neck. He knows to leave his shoes at the top of the step, to pull the door until it clicks, to park his car in the side street the parking attendants will miss, in case it should remain there until the morning. It is a strange appetite I have for him. I've never liked the rough, coarse way he kisses me. His hair feels slightly greasy in my fingers and through the soft linen of this shirt I can feel the paunch of his stomach, filling into the hollow of my waist as he presses his body up against me. But I enjoy the scent of leather from his coat and the eagerness he feels for me. He isn't afraid to make demands on me and it feels sophisticated to be asked for this way. What began as an affair has mellowed into a sweet, familiar medicine. He touches my neck as though it belongs to him and looks often into my eyes.

We first met at a spring tasting dinner, eating pasta with nettles, morels on toast, wild sea trout poached with spinach. Across the round table we found we liked the same wine, lived in the same neighbourhood, ate at the same favourite gastropub with a typewritten menu and mismatched plates. He gave me a ride home and his telephone number, written on the back of a torn-out section of newspaper.

In the beginning we took each other for long, decadent meals, tearing artichokes with our hands, drinking wine and grappa, ending with quick pecks on the cheek. Within weeks we were sitting in his car for hours talking, about the Dogon villages in Mali, the Andalusian farmhouse he is renovating, the pleasure of picking peaches still warm from the sun. It was only later I learned he was famous. I came home and searched through my cookbooks, finding his picture on at least a dozen of the jackets. Typing his name brings up dozens of references to awards, trips to India, Vietnam and Mexico. I found an article describing his Australian wedding as 'the foodie event of the year' and felt a lump in my throat, looking at a photograph of him taken a year before we met, smiling at a crowd of casually dressed, barefoot guests, stirring a blackened cast-iron pot over a wood fire. I used to think he was going to choose me, that we'd live bravely, filling any resulting gulfs with patience and kindness, that the magic potion of romance, understanding and adrenalin was too irresistible to refuse.

Four years later his real wife still lives in France; they are still having problems and I still take his calls. And instead, we lie in bed together planning the trips we'll never take and at the height of our frantic sex, or sometimes afterwards, as I lay in the crook of his ribcage, he tells me that he loves me.

Sometimes, rarely, I tell him that I love him, too. For in those moments I do love him; I love him and I love the simple, familiar combination of us. It is the longevity of that love that has become unimportant. Sometimes it lasts a few days, long enough for a breakfast of kisses, bites of toast, and promises to see more of each other. More often, it fades as he rinses himself in my shower; as I gather up his clothes from where they've scattered on the floor.

They seem enough, those small, random and imperfect moments. Worth being plucked out of my self-centred life for, a few moments at a time. Afterwards, we separate, living in the same city, overlapping, but largely unaware of each other's presence.

Chapter Three

I have never had to wear a hijab. The idea frightens me a little. The shapeless cloak, sombre colours and layers of scarf wrapped around my head and neck; garments so obscuring they seem to create even a laboured, particular walk. At best, I imagine I will look severe and unkind, at worst I fear I may disappear entirely.

I have managed to avoid it until now, even in Yemen. There I had stayed with six women, the Al-Khatib sisters, who wore head-to-toe black, including veils across their faces and dark gloves to cover their hands. Yet each morning as we took turns checking ourselves in the tall mirror that hung in the corridor, they insisted upon my elbow-length sleeves and bare, ponytailed hair. When I tried to cover my head or don a shawl before going outside, they closed in around me, brushing away my attempts, saying, 'No, it is good this way.'

With their fierce swaggers, shrill voices and readiness to

make a scene if something displeased them, they made for powerful guardians as we moved through the narrow, darkened alleys of eastern Sana'a, squashing ourselves onto the creaky public minibuses that took us to the market. I followed the indications of their long, black-covered fingers as they pointed me to a new seat every few stops, a near-constant adjusting and readjusting of places to ensure no woman suffered the indignity of sitting next to a man she wasn't married or related to. As we picked out fish, rabbits or chickens, that squawked and fluttered as they were thrown onto the scales, they whispered warnings of the times they had been insulted by the stray glances and roaming hands of Sana'a's bachelors, who spent much of the afternoon sitting on flattened cardboard boxes in the streets, chewing the handfuls of green hallucinogenic leaves they stuffed into their mouths and wedged in their cheeks.

In their small, white-tiled kitchen the sisters observed a strict pecking order: the youngest and most recently married peeled garlic and scraped carrots while the oldest – twenty-four with three children already – commandeered the groaning Chinese food processor. She fed it handfuls of green chillies, tomatoes and coriander to make the fiery *z'houg* we dipped boiled eggs into for a snack. Under the layers of black cloth that were shed and flung into a corner, the girls revealed the indoor versions of themselves: faded jeans, fitted leggings and baggy sweatshirts saying 'Frankfurt' or 'University of Los Angeles'.

Their skin was smooth and almond-coloured, and their thick hair fell in loose curls around their faces. Their veil-muffled voices became loud and crisp. It felt strangely intimate to see them this way, the shapes and textures of their hair, the red lipstick on their mouths, the fact that some of them preferred pink T-shirts to blue, things few men would ever see.

From morning until midday the Al-Khatib kitchen was a busy hub of reaching arms, tasting spoons and fingers flicking water or oil across eager surfaces. One sister's sizzling pan awaited another's pat of clarified butter and heaping spoonful of *hawaij* spices. A third sister stretched dough across a conical straw pillow while a fourth brushed the surface with beaten egg and scattered sesame seeds. Jars of cardamom were tipped, colanders of rice were washed, and chicken was hacked into neat pieces on a slab of wood balanced on small plastic stools. Unlike their kitchen duties, the care of their ten young children was interchangeable and every mistimed leap over the cushions piled in the living room, demand for a glass of warm milk with rosewater or scorched knee from an overeager approach to the blazing *tanoor* could send any of the sisters running.

I imagine they had expected me to be older and probably lazier but I worked hard for my intrusion into their lives, far beyond the thousand dollars in crisp banknotes that I had paid into the hand of the eldest of the Al-Khatib sons. In exchange for hard currency I had been promised two weeks of being permitted to trail them everywhere they went, and to be placed firmly at the centre of all their cooking and feeding activities. The youngest, who by virtue of being the last born had been spared an early marriage, was enrolled at university and was thrilled to be able to speak English with a native.

Even though they were bound to me by a contractual duty, I sought my right of passage by peeling potatoes and scouring the large battered pots they cooked in, tipping their plastic margarine tubs full of peelings into the sewers that ran fast in the alleyways below. They smiled proudly as I scribbled frantically in my notebook, asking for precision – how much caraway? How many teacups of flour? – determined to translate faithfully the things I had learned and reproduce them on my return home. It wasn't always easy; it was forbidden to photograph even their hands while they tossed dough back and forth until paper thin or checked a fermented batter by pouring it in loose ribbons from a metal ladle. The privacy of their indoor and unwrapped selves was to be guarded and kept hidden at all times.

When their husbands came home for lunch we hid our faces in the kitchen and waited to take their still-warm places on the floor to eat their leftovers. We were smart and always made a surplus of food, feasting on Bedouin-style braised chicken and bubbly buckwheat crêpes soaked in herbed buttermilk. Each meal finished with the golden sesame wafers I adored, pulled hot from the oven and poured with honey bought from the nomads who came into the city twice a year with their full clay jars. When we finally gathered barefoot and hungry around the table-cloth, a blonde girl and a dozen women with headscarves, gold teeth and enough praises for Allah to last until night-fall, we always had enough food to sustain us for the evening ahead.

The lifting and lowering of veils to eat and drink was tedious so staying in was just easier than going out. Evenings saw thirty of us squashed into windowless rooms a quarter of the size of my apartment, to eat sweets, smoke pipes and drink thick tea with cardamom and condensed milk. Children leaped from one lap to another and had their heads patted and their clothes straightened. The youngest waited on the oldest, refreshing cups of tea and offering the largest dates. Each woman, passing through the archway, threw off her covering to reveal elaborate clothing and make-up. A party for a fifteen-year-old second wife (the first wife served the tea and welcomed the guests) featured heavy sequins, big, stiff hair and Cleopatra-style, kohl-lined eyes. Another party celebrating the return of pilgrims from Mecca was a miniature fash-ion show of white, powdered faces and miniskirts. I quickly learned that these parties were more than just a chance to show off; they were a careful sorting exercise to align potential brides with available husbands. The palest girls would go to the wealthiest men and perhaps be taken to live in Russia or Saudi Arabia. The dark-complexioned

girls or those who were cross-eyed were set aside for wid-
owers, second cousins or the poor sons of neighbours who
lived in the villages far away.

In my simple, beaded skirts and unpowdered face I
knew I looked plain to them. I could sense their curiosity and revulsion that I was unmarried and had no
children, perhaps one of those 'open women' they saw on
satellite TV. To compensate they painted my arms and legs
with a black rock they crushed with honey, a mixture that
burned my skin and itched like fleas. Normally used to
adorn new brides for their husbands, it looked strange and
exotic on my pale limbs and I felt a shiver of pleasure on
seeing myself in the mirror. With their approval I took my
place on the floor and I felt an inexplicable longing to
become one of the girls, to be judged solely on the fair-
ness of my complexion, to have my fate defined by my
elders, to be claimed by a man who had never seen my
face. An idea that had always repelled me suddenly seemed
sweet, innocent, even romantic. I was envious of the
clearly defined simplicity that lay ahead of them, the
empty place on the carpet where they would sleep next
to their husbands, the meals cooked to please the family
that would gather around them, and the children who
would cling to their dark sleeves when out of doors,
recognising them by their walk, or a charm worn around
their ankles.

Twice I followed the sisters to the neighbourhood *hammam* where my entrance had to be carefully negotiated.

Amid the passing of ribboned boxes of chocolates and folded banknotes were abundant reassurances to the unsmiling bathhouse attendants that I would tell nothing of the women I saw inside. The privacy of their bodies belonged to them and their husbands, forbidden to the ears of foreign men. To smooth my passage I'd brought a plastic bag filled with European beauty products, conditioners, balms and masks I could arrange neatly, up for grabs beside the steaming buckets of water. In the dim lighting we undressed and changed into the awkward, floor-length, elasticised coverings we wore to wash ourselves, and I closed my eyes to the cockroaches that scurried up and down the damp peeling walls. During those brief, hurried stages of undress I stole envious glances at their bodies, their full breasts and the stretch marks that zigzagged down their thighs. In their company I felt embarrassed by my flat chest, my body unravaged by the efforts of child-bearing and nursing. In a country where women my age looked like mothers, by comparison I felt unutilised, as if I'd been left behind.

But now, as I prepare to go to Iran, putting on a hijab is unavoidable. I am both nervous and excited to wear a scarf in public for the first time. I have been practising at home for over two weeks. Each time I find myself alone I reach for the grey fabric that hangs over the silver knob of the bedroom door.

I try it on in front of the mirror as one might an evening dress or new coat, twisting it with single and double loops around my head to help secure it in place. At first it feels so foreign I can stand to wear it for only a few minutes but gradually I become used to its weight and the constant rustling around my ears. I anticipate how my hair crackles with static each time I remove it, the fabric smelling of my shampoo, the creases in the material softening with wear.

I had hoped I might be a natural, that I'd look breezy and elegant, but it feels strange to smile in clothing so sombre. I pinch my cheeks hard, I pull strands of hair loose, anything to return colour and life to my face. Normally satisfied without make-up, I have a strong urge to wear lipstick. My face seems to scream for rouge. Guided by photographs of Muslim fashion on the internet, I forage through drawers in search of anything to make me feel feminine, trying earrings, eye shadows, decorative clips in my hair.

I test my scarf by walking, running, going up and down stairs, checking its resilience to stay in place. Sometimes I leave one end long enough to drape across my shoulder while other times I flick it around my neck. In some moments I can completely forget its presence, reading a book, typing emails, eating slices of salted cucumbers sitting up in bed, yet talking on the phone or even turning my head quickly can still send it tumbling backwards. Reaching to pull it forward and back into place, a sharp tug of one hand followed by the sweeping motion of the other, is, like my scarf, fast becoming second nature to me.

Each time I remove my scarf I pass it through my

fingers, in awe of what a simple thing it is, the dilemma it poses. The rules from the Iranian embassy are surprisingly unclear, open to bewildering interpretation. 'The headscarf must cover the head and preserve the female's modesty' states the guidance on the reverse of my visa application. But how much hair is allowed to come loose? Which colours are considered modest or daring? What will happen if I cross the line? My enthusiasm at the unfamiliar feel of cloth over my head goes beyond passing the small trials I set for myself: keeping it in place while vacuuming the floor, brushing my teeth, or whipping egg whites into a froth. I feel a childlike anticipation at going to Iran, a place where I know no one, wearing the hijab and making it my own.

Friends shake their heads and feel pity for me, imagining me drab and silent, a shapeless figure among hundreds of other shapeless figures, but I picture myself differently, moving with confidence through crowded Iranian streets. As in my childhood of Catholic school uniforms, where I'd sought to stand out in the line-up at morning assembly or the roll-call in the courtyard, I am discovering again how sparkly jewellery, the removal of a few inches of fabric, the replacement of grey with violet or navy with yellow make a presence more confident and a step more bold. After three years of throwing on jeans and T-shirts, thinking little of whether I was fashionable, my concern isn't the visas, the politics or the danger. All I can think about is what I might wear.

It is not for men that I care how I'll look, but the women I'll be dressing for. I know my choice of clothes will open or shut doors and I am eager to fit in and make friends. I had long learned to identify Iranian women in airports in Paris, Montreal and Dubai, easily distinguishing them from passengers bound for Saudi Arabia, Qatar or other destinations in the Middle East. Standing out in their sunglasses and high heels, with brightly patterned scarves tossed loosely over their hair and clingy designer coats, they seemed more like Mediterraneans – Romans or Catalans – than the dark, hardened images relentlessly shown on the evening news. I admired the gracious way they interacted with each other, queuing in circles instead of lines, speaking loudly and laughing easily, with little regard for personal space.

The first person to see me like this will be the photographer. His studio in a grubby, basement corner of Charing Cross station is no bigger than a bathroom, occupying a cramped unit between a shoe repair shop and a small kiosk selling lottery tickets. Taking a seat on a wooden stool that wobbles when I sit down, I glance at papers taped to the walls showing dimensions for a dozen identity cards and passports, for Australia, South Africa, Schengen visas for Europe. The photographer smiles as he adjusts the position of his camera to allow for my height. He asks me to sit up straight as he pulls down a white canvas behind me. As he reaches over I notice his olive complexion and thick, cotton-wool eyebrows. I worry that perhaps he is Muslim and will find me ridiculous.

I pull out the scarf in my bag, one I've picked just for this occasion. It was bought years ago from the glass cabinet of an expensive shop in Delhi, but has remained for years at the bottom of a drawer, still wrapped in the same peach-coloured tissue paper. It is wide enough to reach to the base of my neck, long enough to go around my head twice. Black, with overlapping gold and silver threads. For reasons I cannot explain, it is important to me, in this first recorded moment of my wearing hijab. I chose this scarf in the hope it will look pretty.

The still-new fabric feels stiff and unyielding as I pass it over my head and under my chin. I am conscious that it must look awkward, sticking up where it should sit flat, but I decline the offer to check myself in the small mirror he gestures to, that hangs from a nail on the wall. I am shy with inexperience and suddenly it feels intimate to be dressing myself in front of a stranger. Instead I turn my head and tilt my chin according to his instructions, waiting for the electronic beeps of the camera to finish before relaxing my face. When the photographs come out I look rigid and doll-like, my hair pressed against my forehead. I accept this is how I will look when my visa is peeled off and stuck into my passport at the Iranian embassy, the photograph surrounded by indecipherable, swirling letters that will spell out my name and birthday, taking up an entire page. It thrills me to imagine seeing my name this way, appearing in a context it feels it doesn't belong in.

I remember the first time I felt that way, when the new telephone directory arrived on my doorstep in Dublin. Thumbing through the fresh paper with ink that stained my fingers black, I found the same surnames repeated, row after row, some spread across several dozen pages. When I finally located mine it struck me as incredible, a single, distinguished, anomalous line. *Klinec J., 1 Longford Terrace, Monkstown.* At the end of the school year I tore out the page, tucking it away in a corner of my suitcase, as if to reassure myself that it hadn't been a dream, a necessary reminder before boarding the plane that took me back to Ontario, to the Buicks and Ford pick-ups, the perfectly straight roads, the air-conditioned buildings of the place I no longer belonged to.

I pack, prepared for the quiet, solitary nights I anticipate, taking cookbooks, a laptop, even workout DVDs and plastic armbands. I expect confinement, evenings when everything will close by 9.30, streets falling silent and inhospitable after dark. With my keys jangling in one hand, I take a final rushed look around the home I am excited to abandon, the neatly made bed, the empty fridge smelling faintly of bleach, the discarded papers tossed into a bin.

There is nothing simple or easy about where I am going. But since I was a student eating my first Persian stew, tearing fibres of lamb between a metal spoon and fork, breathing in the scent of dried black limes, I have chartered a course to this place. It is the pursuit of love that drives me to Iran, a love that has haunted me since I was twenty. It is for love I am willing to sit alone night after night, eating in the empty women's dining rooms of the few restaurants that survived the revolution. It is for love I will weave through the men in crowded, ancient coffeehouses, tolerating the whispering and unashamed stares. It is love that drives me to visit a country cloaked in fear, with a culture much overlooked and long forgotten.

It isn't for monuments, tombs, the great ruins of Persepolis that I will cover my hair and avert my gaze. I am going to Iran for its food.

Not the hunks of skewered lamb on charcoal and raw onions consumed by working men and taxi drivers; I seek instead the food eaten behind closed doors. The long-simmered stews of chicken with golden plums and quince that sustain husbands after long commutes of two bus changes and a shared taxi, or children weary from school lessons where maths and biology are fitted around compulsory modules on morality and the 'history of the Islamic revolution'. I imagine the lamb braised with pomegranate seeds to be eaten after days of biting tongues and swallowing impatience, served with fistfuls of coriander, plucked by women who sit barefoot on carpets. The tough joints braised to falling apart, bought from a carcass purchased by and divided at the local mosque, the cuts of meat handed out at factories in plastic bags to each employee, a gift to celebrate the coming of spring.

I crave food that is important and historical, recipes that have changed little in five hundred years, aside perhaps from the substitution of vegetable oil in place of the sheep's-tail fat that used to be melted down in pans for cooking. I imagine food smelling of the charred insides of battered cooking vessels and the decades-old smoke of earthenware pots, food cooked by generations of women while their children played at their feet and, eventually, while the world as they knew it crashed in around them. I picture tables graced with the taste of proud, complex lives. Herbs carried in special baskets; bread wrapped in knotted, muslin cloths; thick stews soured with unripe grape juice; carrots boiled with sugar and rosewater, yoghurt hung from dripping bags, its whey dried in sheets on trays in the sun. I see the rituals of bread formed by hand, indentations made with fingertips, little hollows shaped to catch pools of oil or broth.

It's true: what I seek is largely romance, the legacy of a country where women are compared to food – her breasts like pomegranates, her lips like ripe dates. I am charmed by the notion of families tucking their feet under a single low table, gathering under blankets to eat slices of watermelon and feta sweetened with rosewater, listening to stories recounted by grandparents. I see myself trespassing as if a character in a work of historical fiction, chasing the last shreds of scorched meat and caramelised sauce from the sides of iron pans, eating spoonfuls of resinous, saffron-speckled ice cream, the latter stretching magically from bowl to mouth in long, chewy strands.

I have precise ambitions, one more specific than all. I want to eat that most famous of Iranian delicacies: I want to eat Iranian rice.

Iranian rice is unlike any other. It isn't boiled or steamed or thrown unceremoniously into a rice cooker. Iranian rice is first soaked and bathed like a Hindu princess, rinsed in three changes of just-warm water. It goes into the pot with a spoonful of salt, carefully simmered just until it begins to yield, its determined character and bite remaining intact. Finally it is drained and returned to the pot in a footpool of melted butter, over the gentlest of heat, until it is so impossibly light and fluffy it could fill the quilts and pillows of Buckingham Palace.

Tipped out into a wide, shallow serving bowl, each grain of rice is perfectly separate and served piled high like wedding confetti, adorned with streaks of bright yellow saffron and dotted with a final, loving pat of yet more butter. But the best part of all is still to come: the *tahdig*. A crisp, buttery, golden crust of rice left to scorch on the bottom of the pan to just the right thickness, the *tahdig* is shattered into gem-like shards and scattered on top of the rice. It crunches and crackles and splinters in your mouth as you eat.

Apparently, in Iran you could go to a restaurant and order a whole, luxuriant dish of nothing but *tahdig*, and I want to do exactly that.

It is a long way from London to this place I long for, where I can untangle myself from everything. To Iran I was taking all my romantic ideas. I was bringing the best, kindest version of myself. In turn I hoped the best, most beautiful parts of Iran might reveal themselves to me.

Chapter Four

His 'hello' was more of a bark than a greeting and I'd expected him to be older when I glanced up from my book. He'd placed a hand across his eyes, squinting in the late afternoon sun to look at me. He had a broad nose and fine, sharp cheekbones, offset by long, almost feminine eyelashes, features I suppose could have been handsome if I'd stopped to consider them. But all I noticed was his distant expression and his mouth, how it seemed fixed permanently into a scowl. I guessed he was probably in his late twenties, yet his face was so stern it was hard to guess. He was wearing a white cotton shirt with an American-style collar and dark, loose-fitting jeans with wide pockets – the kind that seemed popular with young Iranian men; jeans made in Turkey but labelled 'Italy'.

I don't imagine he approached me out of anything but boredom. I wasn't even a person then, just a foreigner. A *khaareji.* I belonged to the trickle of fair-complexioned visitors who passed through his city on the edge of the desert, marvelling at the walls made of packed clay and straw, tracing their hands along them as they walked through the old laneways around the bazaar.

He began to question me, quickly but without enthusiasm, scarcely waiting for my answers before starting his next question. I sensed he was speaking more for the enjoyment of hearing his own voice in English than anything to do with talking to me. He'd later tell me he often approached tourists to practise, but had never seen a foreign girl, sitting alone.

'Where are you from?'

'What is your idea about Iran?'

'What have you seen so far in our country?'

Each time I answered he watched me critically, his eyes narrow and his face unsmiling. I looked down at my watch to check the time, thinking I'd give him five more minutes, at most.

He didn't know that I'd arrived in his country only nine hours earlier. That just a day before I'd been looking at pictures of his city in a guidebook. That only that morning I'd woken up in Mehrabad airport, waiting for the Tupolev plane that would bring me here. Probably he would have laughed if I'd told him my first reaction to Iran had been fear. The wailing call to prayer that had filled the airport had been so shrill I'd instinctively drawn my knees in. That red-faced, man-boy, cry-singing sound, distorting and crackling in the dusty speakers that hung from wires, had closed in on me like a dense fog.

The thick carpeting in the airport had smelled of damp and the air-conditioning was on too high, causing me to shiver. All around me people – men with blank faces and large, tightly wrapped women – shuffled their way to the designated prayer rooms in the corner clutching over-stuffed plastic cases and yellowed travelling pillows. From the corners of their bags poked gold-lettered packages of regional sweets – sticky pistachio nougat from Esfahan, honey and saffron brittle from Qom – gifts that would likely be tipped onto oval serving plates and passed around later that evening with tea.

The row of seats along the amber-tinted window where I'd sat, packed with businessmen and families just moments before, had emptied. I'd heard the call to prayer many times before – in Istanbul, in Damascus, in the graffiti streets around East London – but never so cold and piercing as that. The cheap tinny echo and the severe, red-faced distortions: I could feel them as if they were vibrating between my teeth.

I reached up and realised that my scarf had slipped off my head while I'd been sleeping. With a sense of panic, I yanked it sharply back into place and peered around the terminal, expecting reproach. I rubbed my eyes and felt the gritty residue of the mascara I had applied carefully the previous evening – wanting to look nice for my trip, my first-ever trip to Iran – crumble between my fingers.

A man with sunglasses perched on top of his thick, gelled hair sat facing me on the opposite side of the room. I could feel him staring at me and knew enough not to look up. I didn't need him to come and sit next to me, to hear dull stories about visiting his cousin in Germany, or to anticipate the moment when he'd misread my lack of inhibition and lean in, perhaps putting his hand on my knee and thinking that it was because of him that I was confident and open, a relaxed kind of girl.

It made no sense then, that I should have treated him differently, this stranger who now approached me in Yazd, that I nodded when he asked if he could sit down. Perhaps I recognised the same lack of interest I felt towards him, reflected in his indifference and the physical distance he maintained between us. I failed to warm to him when he told me his name was Vahid, that he'd learned English in school, that he had studied to be an engineer. He'd stood with his arms folded across his chest, making me wonder if maybe he was nervous. His long fingers reached down and twisted the loose cords of the rug covering the wooden bench next to mine. Every third sentence he ran his hand through his coarse, dark hair, his voice so flat it came across more like a lecture. He spoke rusty, disjointed English and I supposed I could have tried to make it easier, to anticipate his sentences, help him find the right words, but his gruff, invasive manner stopped me; I preferred to let him struggle.

He possessed none of the ease in speaking with girls I

associated with men who approached tourists in the Middle East. There were no pre-practised lines, no self-assured script, no leading to an eventual hope of a tryst without consequence. Instead it was as if speaking to me was a breach of his confidence. I suspect he'd been long accustomed to being coddled by the women of his life – his mother and his aunts – where his voice had been loudest and his opinions widely sought, even on matters where he understood little. Perhaps speaking to me as he did then, had forced him onto unfamiliar ground.

It was only when he was joined by his uncle, an older, smiling version of him, that I began to relax. By the simple fact of living in exile, with one foot planted in the soil of each of our worlds, his uncle's presence created a bridge between us. His uncle explained how three decades ago he'd left Iran for Pennsylvania at the outbreak of the Iran–Iraq war; and was coming back now for a visit, without his American wife and children who'd refused to accompany him. A 'Not without my daughter complex', he joked.

They'd spent the afternoon together scouring the bazaar for souvenirs, pieces of jade jewellery to please his teenage daughters. To Vahid's disappointment, his uncle could no longer tolerate the intense heat and the dust, leading him to remember the place where I too had stopped to rest, having grown weary of exploring his city on foot. The cafe of my hotel was where he first approached me, a converted merchant's house that had once sheltered a family of twenty. I'd ordered tea and sought out a quiet table in the courtyard where I could sit undisturbed, a sail-like canopy billowing overhead. I don't recall which I'd found more beautiful: the turquoise-tiled fountains and amber stained glass of my surroundings or the assortment of sugar that arrived on the silver tea tray. The yellow rock sugar that looked like amethysts, the jagged white lump sugar dusted with sediment, which he'd later show me was chiselled from a torpedo-shaped hunk using tools resembling ice picks. The two men kicked off pairs of sturdy leather shoes and stretched out on the wooden daybed beside mine, expertly placing two lumps of sugar on their tongues. Biting down with just the right pressure, they raised glasses of tea to their mouths, sipping it through the sugar, sweetening the tea as it passed through their lips.

Observing them I quickly saw the difference between the Iranians in Iran and those who had emigrated. Vahid's questions were direct and intrusive while his uncle's were gentler and more discreet. It was a distinction I'd first become aware of at Heathrow, on joining the check-in queue with my one small bag, stepping in amongst the luggage trolleys piled with suitcases coated in plastic film. The gathering of people had already attained the semblance of Iran, adopted its clear and unspoken rules. Old came before young, parents before children, elaborate Persian greetings before brief English ones. Suitcases were stuffed with presents, strangers greeted with handshakes;

conversations lingered on the latest round of sanctions and its effects on the price of bread and petrol. Young children were hoisted into the air.

For some the check-in had seemed routine, even blasé, as they fished their maroon passports out of purses and pockets, carefully separating them from the black, navy or green ones from their adopted countries. Others appeared more tense, less sure. It was the little things – the inability to hold eye contact, the chewing of gum, the affected, disinterested stances – that suggested a vulnerable footing between East and West. I imagine these are the Iranians who might cover their faces when protesting at the embassy, or use false names in their Facebook accounts; who may have experienced their first taste of physical intimacy abroad, liberated from worrying about their reputations. I imagine how a return to Iran would cause them to chafe and feel agitated, how everything that could be counted as a milestone could be turned against them. They wore their best clothes purchased from Lacoste and Benetton to go home in, even knowing they would be compelled to give their coats and jackets away, to the cousins who would envy them and pay them compliments.

Vahid had been surprised to learn I had come alone, that it had been my second attempt at getting a visa, that I was already thirty-one, older than him. He saw the Persian cookbook open next to me and I began to tell him about my life in London, three and a half thousand miles away. He'd seemed intrigued that I ran my own business, was independent, I think it was the first time I saw him smile. Having just completed two years of military service, he seemed to find it incredible that someone could exert such a degree of control over their life. 'Tell me all the countries you have been to,' he'd asked. Slowly one by one I recited a list, pausing while he tried to remember the Persian names for Ethiopia, Mozambique, small islands in the Caribbean. Sometimes we drew maps with our fingers on the carpets we sat on, tracing the outlines of continents to help him locate the places I mentioned. I could feel him glance at me for longer periods and his face became relaxed, almost handsome.

Encouraged by his attention I told him of my reason for coming to Iran, of the things I was excited to cook and taste.

I expected him to be impressed with my knowledge, that I knew the foods his city was famous for. I looked for him to smile when I mentioned *shooli*, a soup of beetroot and vinegar thickened with flour, and tiny Yazdi cakes made with ground rice and pistachios.

'My mother is a good cook,' was all he said.

'Would she be willing to spend time with me and let me watch her?' I ventured finally.

'Well, we'll have you ask her,' he'd replied, his voice betraying an irritation that surprised me. His expression again became cool and uninterested, and I didn't know what to make of him. The momentary kindness disappeared and he seemed to tense up, a scowl returning to his face.

I had to admit to myself it was easier to go out accompanied by him. When I'd first arrived, I'd been fit for little more than sleep. I'd collapsed exhausted on the hard bed in my room, after briefly taking in its low ceilings and dark, stained-glass windows, and dropping my bags onto the patchwork of carpets strewn across the floor. I'd been intimidated later emerging into the blinding sunlight. The streets around the bazaar were narrow, amplifying the sound of mopeds roaring past. At least three times teenage boys pretended to trip in an excuse to brush up against me. Unsure of how to begin, I started walking, guided by glances at a map I'd torn from my guidebook. I stopped to buy ice cream in a paper cup with carrot juice poured over, gesturing to a cardboard menu written in black marker in English. It was the first thing I tasted in his country. It reminded me of the orange creamsicles my sister and I devoured as children, the carrot juice sweet and vibrant instead of bitter and watery like it was at home.

I followed a group of chattering schoolchildren onto the rooftop of a mosque and gazed out over the straight roads, the narrow strips of grass where small groups of young men and families sprawled on blankets, the woodsmoke of their makeshift barbecues rising up to the sky.

I looked out and watched the women who hurried along the pavements in his city, wearing severe, black cloaks pulled forward to their eyebrows, with children scurrying close behind. I remembered what I'd read about the place he came from, that despite living in a city known for the sensuous curves of its adobe passages and romantically named alleyways, the occupants of Yazd – the Yazdi – were famous for being conservative and financially shrewd. That the men dressed in peasant clothes and cheap plastic sandals but were secretly rich, renowned for their furious bargaining skills. That transactions at the market, at the rice seller, in the narrow archways of the gold bazaar, were belaboured exchanges of tuts and hisses, whispered offers with lowered eyes, counter-offers protested while patting empty wallets in pockets. That upon agreeing a suitable price, buyer and seller would shake hands three times, and reach into stashes of tightly rolled banknotes tucked into nylon socks or secret compartments hand-sewn into underpants.

It had raised eyebrows on the plane when I stated it as my first destination. 'Yazd?!' The couple who'd sat in front of me on the flight had looked at me as if it were the moon. Like most of my fellow passengers they shunned the provinces, preferring the tree-lined suburbs of northern Tehran. They were joined by four or five others who laughed, taking turns imitating the dialect and excessive courtesies spoken by the inhabitants of his city, the showering of *ta'arof* phrases used to conduct business or exchange pleasantries. 'I am your servant,' 'May your hand not ache,' 'I sacrifice myself for you!' they'd mimicked in clipped Yazdi accents.

Even the weddings of the Yazdi were famous within

Iran, they'd insisted. I'd heard how when Yazdi marry, the wedding guests follow the newly married couple in their walk to their new home while a family friend or relative reads out the list of wedding presents. The aunt of the bride has bought the couple a new washing machine! The Zahedi family have given a new rug! With the announcement of each gift, the wedding spectators would clap and cheer loudly and it was the couple's job to blush their unworthiness. The Yazdi women, meanwhile, made careful observations and scribbled down a quiet tally of the new bounty in little black books. In Yazd, the economics of gift-giving were taken very seriously, with any imbalances painstakingly noted and redressed at future occasions, down to the nearest Rial.

I wanted to tell him about my plane journey, where I'd first learned the folklore of his city, and how I'd been shocked to find I was the only non-Iranian on board. I wanted to describe the voracious appetites of the other passengers, consuming copious glasses of wine and miniature bottles of vodka, supplementing the meagre quantities of food with foil-wrapped pouches of bread and nets of oranges, apples eaten straight through including the cores. I wanted to tell him about the young man next to me who had spilled dozens of photographs into my lap, snapshots of available cousins for him to consider for marriage. How I'd felt faintly repulsed by their complexions thickly covered in white foundation and overplucked eyebrows replaced with crayon-like streaks of eyeliner. Their photos circulated several rows ahead and behind us, with everyone offering advice on who seemed the best choice.

I wanted to tell him of the discarded sunflower seeds and peanut shells that had rained down onto the carpet, that it had been the most fun I'd had on a plane in my life. How I'd felt a thrilling anxiety when the plane began its descent to Khomeini airport and the pilot announced that all ladies' clothing must conform to the dress code of the Islamic Republic of Iran before disembarking. I wanted to describe for him the eerie choreography of the women reaching en masse into their purses and handbags for scarves and draping them over their heads. I wanted to tell him how later, once we'd arrived in the terminal, I'd stood and watched my fellow passengers be swallowed up by the crowd pressed against the viewing glass, a swollen mass of black cloaks and dark eyes, and had felt terrified of finding myself alone here, beneath the enormous, lifelike painting of Ayatollahs Khomeini and Khamenei with their unsmiling faces and long, white beards.

But instead of sharing these details I told him nothing of my first movements in his country. I told him nothing and he didn't seem to care.

His uncle stood up and asked if I'd like to join them on their evening's sightseeing and Vahid looked neither pleased nor disappointed when I accepted. 'Iran is very safe, safer than America' was only thing he said to acknowledge my decision, digging his hands into his pockets.

I don't know why I agreed to accompany them. Perhaps it was the lure of speaking after uttering no more than a handful of sentences the entire afternoon. Probably because I felt safer, adjusting to Iran in their presence. I wondered whether perhaps Vahid had pitied for me, if he'd found it sad to see me there all alone. I detested the idea that he should feel sorry for me or feel obligated to take me on as a charity project.

As we walked towards his father's car he stepped in front of me to lead the way, across roads with little traffic, through junctions with only a handful of people. He crossed the street with the traffic always to his left, shunting me to his right, making himself into a shield. His father's car; he'd insisted on reversing and turning towards the direction of traffic before stepping out and ushering me inside. Though his chivalry was excessive, I went along with it, digging a space for myself among the jackets and Kleenex boxes strewn across the back seat.

As he drove he spoke in English so as not to exclude me. He addressed his uncle as 'Uncle', which to me sounded strangely aristocratic. Possibly even to him it felt odd and imprecise, compared to *dayii*, the term he would normally have used, making it clear even to strangers that this was his mother's brother. He was a good driver, confident and relaxed, and even when he took his eyes off the road temporarily to reach for a CD I felt unconcerned. Without realising it he gave me my first taste of joy, reuniting me with the textures of the Middle East, the structure of traffic I loved where three lanes became five, where cars veered up alongside each other. I was so close I could almost touch the men whose hands clenched around the steering wheels, the women who hunched in the back with babies in their arms, the tassels that swayed from the rolls of gilded, laminated fabric tacked across the tops of dashboards. Occasionally he drove up on the pavements, his wing mirrors only millimetres away from scraping along buildings, and I found it thrilling to watch pedestrians rush from his path. Cars blasted their horns at regular intervals, a kind of sonar to warn each other of their approach.

He parked outside a mosque lit up for the evening prayers and I heard the last notes of the *azoon* crackling through speakers. Men and women streamed through the turquoise and indigo arches carrying their shoes, striding across the tiled inner courtyard. By now Vahid had switched into speaking in Farsi, walking with his uncle, their arms around each other. I was happiest simply retreating behind them. They took turns glancing back at me, checking to see whether I'd fallen behind, pausing for me when I'd stopped to watch people washing their feet under brass taps, patting dampened hands to their heads, smoothing their hair. At the entrance to the mosque men stepped gingerly onto the patterned carpet, reaching for prayer mats, while the women scurried past a thick green curtain. It billowed softly each time a female figure rushed past, anchored by the soft folds of material bunched together on the floor.

I was mortified when Vahid offered me a chador from a musty pile near the doorway, encouraging me to join the women inside. But my confidence was still thrown after my shaky arrival and I was convinced I would make a fool of myself.

'It's ok,' he'd said. 'They'll be happy to see you.' But I shook my head, backing away. He shrugged his shoulders and tossed the robe into the pile, again turning his back to me.

When afterwards he dropped me at my hotel he'd insisted on walking me to the door. His uncle waited in the car, leaving us for a second time alone together. We retraced the two hundred yards in relative silence, still strangers to one another, pausing only at the approach of mopeds where he insisted I stand behind him. For reasons I can't explain I wasn't hugely curious about him. He was bossy and aloof. I suspected he might be an only child. I'd been surprised later to learn that he had a sister, but equally unsurprised to discover he was the only son. His vigilance and jostling made me feel frustrated with him – struck me as at odds with what I'd told him about myself; to the point where once I'd purposely ignored him and walked in another direction, leaving him calling after me.

On reaching the thick wooden door of my hotel I'd been surprised when he reached his hand to me, shocked when he scribbled his name and address onto a page in his notebook and tore it out, pressing it into my hand.

'Call me tomorrow at one p.m.,' he'd said, still without smiling.

Watching him retreat down the narrow pathway, I was unsure whether I would call him at all.

Chapter Five

Vahid waits for me at the entrance gate, his face unshaven, his hair messy and crumpled with sleep. He is wearing a hooded grey sweatshirt that looks as if it has been pulled over his head at the last minute and a pair of sunglasses dangle from his hand. Behind him stands the apartment complex where he lives with his parents, a cluster of sand-coloured brick buildings about four storeys high.

His flat expression comes as no surprise to me. I know already to expect it. When I'd phoned from the taxi, defeated by his illegible handwriting, the casual tone of his voice made me think I'd misunderstood his invitation. I'd passed my phone to the driver so Vahid could explain the whereabouts of his address. When he finished he'd hung up, without asking to speak to me again. He didn't think to tell me it was a further twenty minutes away or to watch for the beautiful old henna mill we'd pass. Instead

I leaned my head back against the cracked leather seat, breathing in the hot, stale air. It all felt bewildering to me to be driving this far across the city, towards the address that flaps gently in my hand. Bewildering, I thought to myself, opening the window a crack, that this is my first day waking up in Iran.

As we pull up to the curb, he pokes his head in the window and argues with the driver about the fare. 'You paid too much,' he grumbles, passing me the banknote he retrieves on my behalf.

I follow him past the guards into a wide courtyard planted neatly with flowering shrubs. Several small children pour water into a makeshift hole and fashion sculptures from sandy soil packed into sawed-off tin cans. Two *chadori* women, dressed in long, dark shrouds, chat while rustling plastic shopping bags, their deep, masculine voices sounding urgent despite the midday heat. Vahid melts into something boyish and gentle in their presence, enquiring after their health, his voice rising several octaves higher than it has ever done with me. Above our heads the windows of the apartments are blacked out with amber adhesive panels, frayed and peeling around the edges. The balconies are concealed more vibrantly with colourful sheets – bright paisley patterns, elaborate equestrian scenes – generously strung from sagging lengths of twine and tightly wound around black iron railings: the miniature worlds behind them are betrayed by faint glimpses of an upended mop or a haphazard clothesline, the swishing of rubber flip-flops, the scratching of a corn broom.

Vahid leads me to a wide, communal stairway, yawning loudly as we make our way up the four flights of stairs, past the plastic trays piled with shoes, the little wooden cabinets stacked neatly with shoehorns and tins of polish. As we pass each doorway I wonder about the secret women dwelling behind them. I imagine them relaxing while their husbands are at work, sprawled across maroon velvet sofas, feet up, relishing taking up entire spaces usually crammed with relatives and children. Perhaps they are watching Korean soap operas and eating ice cream, or polishing toenails while gossiping on the phone, twirling their long, loose hair around their fingers. Vahid presses a doorbell on the fourth-floor landing and I recognise the dark brown shoes he wore the day before, placed neatly against the wall, toes pointing outwards. Instead of a chime, the doorbell plays a metallic version of 'All You Need is Love'. I can't help but smile at the strangeness of hearing it here, a Lennon–McCartney composition, in this building with its opaque windows, its inhabitants with their muted knowledge of one another, in this country where all Western music is banned.

Unlike Vahid, his mother looks as if she's been up for hours and opens the door in a way that instantly makes me feel wanted. She seems nervous but excited as she steps aside to let us pass, her face kind and smiling, her manner calm and unhurried. The full-length black cloak she wears brushes the tops of her feet, her matching scarf a tight loop around her head. A faint line of black pencil is smudged under her eyes and modest, silver jewellery clatters at her wrists and earlobes. She asks Vahid to fetch a crystal vase, its weight too much for her slight build, and fills it with water, dropping into it the flowers I give her, together with a spoonful of sugar. Methodically she pinches off wilted leaves with her fingers, tossing them into a plastic bowl of spent tea leaves next to the sink. She instructs Vahid to place the flowers on a low table in the centre of the living room, a gesture of politeness, to show she likes the small gift I've brought.

I take the cup of tea she offers to me on a tray and step from the carpet onto the linoleum floor. Her kitchen is bright and compact with large red cabinets, work surfaces covered in lace doilies and plastic flowers. By its gleaming door I understand the oven has never been used, filled instead with books, plastic vials of prescription medicines and bags of cotton wool. I suspect it is a consequence of the inhospitable climate that this is not a part of the country where chickens are roasted or casseroles are baked. Such heat-intensive cooking is likely carried out over a fire outdoors.

On the rim of the extractor fan stands an assembly of evil eyes, prayer verses and a smiling porcelain cat wearing the label 'Pennsylvania, USA'. Mindful not to disturb its careful order, I empty my Iranian cookbooks onto her countertop and she leans across to open them. She flips through the pages, tracing her fingers over the colour photographs, murmuring the names of recipes written in both English and Persian. Vahid leans in to supervise but steps away after five minutes, both bored and redundant in our universal language of food. He seats himself in front of the television, opening a laptop, with a stack of engineering textbooks scattered next to him on the floor. Occasionally he returns to the kitchen to pluck a banana or orange from a wicker basket but his entrances and exits go largely unnoticed.

At first Vahid's mother assumes I know nothing, can't even boil an egg, astonished a Western girl could eat anything other than spaghetti and hamburgers. She believes she is teaching me to cook from scratch and as a result gives me only the simplest things to do. As we prepare the afternoon meal of *ash e reshteh* – a thick, herbal porridge with dark wheat noodles – I know she can't imagine such a meal would be considered time-consuming in London: the simmering of dried chickpeas too laborious; the washing of bundles of dill, parsley and coriander too cumbersome; the dried mint from her window ledge she crumbles between her palms into a pan of frothing butter too rich and intense.

During the two hours we spend breaking noodles into fragrant, bubbling pots and turning herb and pistachio omelettes with only our fingers, I come to understand she is in every way a mother. She pauses instinctively for me to watch her reconstitute sun-dried balls of whey with water, rubbing them with her hands in a ceramic bowl. She leans in close to observe my face as she holds out the resulting *kashk*, anticipating a grimace when the salty tang hits my tongue. She secures the stove by turning pot handles inwards before handing me a wooden spoon to brown some onions. I can easily imagine her teaching a young Vahid to tie his shoelaces and comb his hair, to recite prayers or fold newspaper covers around his schoolbooks. More than once she refers to me as *teflaki*, an empathy used for people who are fragile, vulnerable in her eyes because I am alone.

On the days that follow I return to her kitchen, where we stand barefoot side by side. I can tell she finds my interest slightly excessive, unaccustomed to such involvement in the activities of her kitchen, the routine she conducts without even thinking. They are as much a part of her as the prayers she excuses herself for, changing into a blue and white gown, turning towards the direction of Mecca, pressing her forehead to the ground. In her I sense the same strain of capability I recognise in myself; the meat she pulls from her freezer – the chicken legs portioned exactly for *fesenjun*, the fish steaks with black skin that will feed precisely four. Like me she enjoys her rice with extra salt, is unashamed to enjoy the taste of her own cooking, picks at the last slices of raw onion from a serving plate with her fingers.

She begins to look to me for compliments, unaccustomed to praise, teaching me words to describe our food as delicious; to accept her wishes of 'nectar for your soul' at the end of each meal. I feel a mutual fondness emerge between us, but she is careful it never strays into the maternal, an invisible line having been drawn. She reciprocates the hand I rest on her shoulder, the goodbye kisses I place on her cheeks, but her attention to me remains solicitous and formal, keeping me always at a thoughtful distance.

Secretly I am grateful to be spared the cloying affection she heaps upon her family: the husband who addresses her as 'madame' in my presence and the son she dotes upon like a small child. I avert my eyes when she places cushions under their heads or removes socks from their feet, tossing them into a heap. Once after dinner she stroked Vahid's hair with her fingers, murmuring and cooing while she massaged his scalp. He leaned his head back as if accustomed to it, and I found myself feeling mildly repulsed. Perhaps sensing I was watching Vahid opened his eyes and, as if conscious of my thoughts, shook her off immediately, looking embarrassed, rising from his place on the floor.

Each morning as I arrive and pass through their doorway I am hopeful of being urged to remove my scarf and coat, knowing the invitation to 'be free' must come from Vahid's mother. I hope it may come as our intimacy grows, earned through the skinning of broad beans, the paring of turnips, the sorting of wheat kernels for tiny stones. Or the moments our elbows touch as I stand next to her at the stove and wait for the shimmer of walnut oil to rise to the surface and the pot of rice that must return to the boil after the addition of three tea glasses of cold water. I feel my face flushing with the warmth of the kitchen, my clothes growing damp with perspiration beneath my coat, my scarf carrying the odour of frying oil when I finally remove it at the end of the day.

It is only when Vahid suggests I look hot and uncomfortable that she takes any notice of my red face. She says something quickly to him, sounding annoyed and sharp, and goes to her daughter's bedroom where I hear the opening and closing of a chest of drawers. She returns carrying a long, cotton nightdress, offering it for me to wear, a puzzled expression on her face. Trying it on, I feel silly in the teddy-bear pattern and frilly bows, amazed a twenty-three-year-old would wear such a thing. But I am relieved to exchange it for my dark coat and scarf, eager for the opportunity to bare my arms and hair. I suspect, as I return to the kitchen, this is how Vahid's parents imagine all unmarried girls should be – dressed in pink and yellow, covered in ribbons, living in a world where the dour, profound colours of black, brown or grey have yet to set in.

By the end of the day she too has removed her scarf and seems to take pleasure in seeing me comfortable. She puts it back on only when I take photographs and without so much black I begin to find her pretty. She wears about the same amount of make-up as me and with unobstructed views we openly analyse each other. She marvels at the extent of the blonde streaks in my hair and I notice how she gathers her thin curls into a bun. One day when I arrive with a dusting of blusher on my cheeks she mistakes it for sunburn and tells her daughter on the phone I am 'thin-skinned' and not made for the harsh desert sun. She describes how I wander freely in their home without my scarf, seeming proud at how liberal she has become. I don't realise, perhaps none of us does, that I am slowly entering their private, inner world. With this one gesture, I have crossed from *zahir* to *batin*, from the public into the circle where Iranians open their hearts. It is in this world they show affection and share troubles, freed from the need to maintain distance and appearances. As the days pass I feel I belong to them, hearing my name punctuating their sentences, my place in their home clearly defined. After five days it feels as if I live here. Strange that I could have anywhere else to go.

Each evening, Vahid is tasked with taking me back to my hotel. Unlike the morning journey that I make alone, the return is a series of rushed walks through crowded *meidans* and scuffles from one shared taxi to the next.

I don't enjoy travelling with him. Vahid is brusque and impatient, resuming his pattern of shoving me first to one side and then the other, positioning himself between me and the night-time traffic. The only thing I like is that he edits nothing, steers nothing indelicate out of my path. Instead of Yazd's wide boulevards and tree-lined avenues, we traverse guttered alleys and deafening laneways, neigh-bourhoods where doors are left ajar. We pass homes where women squat on the floors folding laundry into baskets, barber shops where moustaches are trimmed and hair is oiled. Beneath our feet pools of sheep and chicken blood coagulate in the sun, sparks fly out from darkened garages where rusted metal is fused together.

Unlike the streets in London, where couples would be out for the evening, energetic, holding hands or kissing, with their arms around each other, the few couples I spot seem languid and tired; most have one or two small children in tow.

As in the afternoons I spend in the kitchen with his mother while he lies on the floor largely oblivious to me, Vahid and I also form a routine. I achieve very few words in his presence, the opposite of how we each spend our days. He has just completed two years of military service and seems to prefer talking at rather than to me, probably to avenge the two years he's just spent being ordered around. He points out monuments, mosques and ruins, telling me extensively about their histories, failing to notice when I am distracted or lack interest.

Sometimes as we walk, Vahid points out girls, asking whether I think they are beautiful. 'Iranian girls are the most beautiful in the world,' he declares. 'When I marry I will choose only the most beautiful girl. It is very impor-tant!' As he speaks I can see the baldness he inherited from his father advancing across his scalp.

One afternoon Vahid's mother and I finish early and instead of taking me directly home Vahid leads me to a large, outdoor garden. He suggests we stop for tea, saying the words more as a command than a question, never considering that I might refuse. The place he has chosen is surrounded by pomegranate trees with ornate pavements and small brass lanterns to be lit up at night. Husbands take photographs of their wives and children in front of a fountain and call out to the boys who rush back and forth, carrying trays of tea and wrinkly, black dates. We sit at opposite ends of a large wooden bench covered in rugs and pillows; a spot more suited to a courting couple than to the two of us who have nothing to say. Families at neighbouring tables turn to look across at us, whispering unsubtly behind cupped hands.

'You are my cousin, OK?' Vahid says. 'If anyone asks.'

'Sure, OK,' I nod.

'Your mother's sister and my father's brother are married and live in the US.'

'Got it,' I reply.

Our tea arrives and as we sit, saying little, the feeling of being scrutinised begins to unnerve me. The right thing to do is to try to speak to him, to appear familiar, but I feel separate from him in every possible way. The sole tie that binds us is his mother and her kitchen, and the meals I watch disappear down his throat. If my daily presence in his house seems even vaguely novel to him, he gives very little away. He always seems distant, absorbed in faraway things; his prickliness feels as if it would take months to break down.

Though the wooden benches are spaced several metres apart, families crowd the free places on either side of us, instructing their teenagers to listen in and translate the few words that pass between us. I look at Vahid, expecting him to be irritated, but he seems unconcerned, even pleased by the attention. I wonder whether he has brought me here just to show off. Two girls of university age approach shyly, asking me questions, and although our conversation is trite, I am thankful for the diversion. When they depart Vahid is stirring sugar into his third glass of tea, one leg tucked under his body, a brooding expression on his face.

He turns to me finally. 'Are you a virgin?'

'No, of course not!' I answer immediately without thinking. I feel more horrified by the suggestion, which feels so absurd, than by the blunt intrusion into my privacy. I know I should be angry, even insulted, by his question, but this sudden flash of humanness has caught me off guard. Vahid stares down at his hands folded in his lap, looking bizarrely vulnerable and boyish. I can tell he rarely speaks to girls, especially about anything as intimate as sex.

Conscious of the families all around us, I lower my voice to a whisper. 'Something would have had to have gone very wrong in my life for me to still be a virgin.'

'I will stay a virgin until I get married,' he replies stiffly, puffing out his chest in self-righteousness.

'Really? And when do you plan to get married?'

'Not until I am at least thirty-five. Girls just distract men from their ambitions so I want to get married late.'

I try to imagine scenes of Vahid and his future wife, a pair of thirty-something virgins fumbling clumsily on their wedding night. I'm unsure which is harder to picture: staying a virgin until thirty-five or Vahid connecting emotionally with any girl enough to get her to sleep with him.

'But what if you die tomorrow?' I persist. 'Won't you feel like you have missed out on something?'

Vahid looks at me, clearly shocked. I feel oddly victorious at seeing him so unsettled.

He stares into the distance, his eyebrows furrowed, and again we return to sitting without speaking. We drain our glasses of tea in silence, the sun moving lower, until he turns, abruptly picking up his jacket.

'We should go,' he says in a low voice. 'It's getting late.'

The next day I wake up, dreading going back, lingering in bed for the first morning since I arrived. Instead of racing to the courtyard to eat a breakfast of warm bread, sliced peaches and cherry jam, I contemplate making up an excuse, forming alternative plans in my head. It should be easy enough, I tell myself – I am unwell, sick, have a stomach ache. There are places I can visit, monuments I've read about. Who goes to a city and sees only the inside of a kitchen? When the phone eventually rings I nearly ignore it, knowing it is well after eleven, the time I would be normally be reaching for a plastic colander, a knife from the drawer. Vahid's voice has only the faintest trace of awkwardness. What time am I coming? When will I be there?

An hour later I ring the doorbell but no smells are emerging into the hallway. When Vahid opens the door I see that he is alone at home.

'My mom teaches religious Arabic on Wednesday mornings. Both my parents are out, but they suggested I take you sightseeing.'

For the sake of his mother I trail him reluctantly down the stairs, through the open courtyard, and out past the entry gates. Vahid doesn't think to tell me where we are going and by now I am used to his lack of commentary. I know I am expected to follow him without question. I have become his family's responsibility and am under his charge. As awkward as it is, I no longer take offence as I did at the beginning, conscious that in a few more days I will leave Yazd and be free again. I allow myself to fall naturally to his right as we traverse the straight roads, to stand behind the arm he raises saying 'Wait' before crossing.

As we walk along a dusty path towards two rocky hills, I feel the lingering effects of yesterday's awkward conversation. We say almost nothing as we walk together, our shoes kicking up small clouds of dust. I have made up my mind to pretend it never happened, and am hoping he will do the same.

'I couldn't sleep at all last night,' he blurts out suddenly.

'I kept thinking about what you said to me. It was going around and around in my mind.'

It is not my intention to comfort or reassure him, so I turn my head away and pretend not to hear.

We reach the base of the pair of hills and I recognise where we are at once. It is the old Zoroastrian *dakhmeh* I had read about, special hilltop structures known as the Towers of Silence. They had been used up until the late 1960s by the Zoroastrians for laying out their dead.

Vahid begins to tell me the history of these places, of the Zoroastrians who didn't believe in burials. Instead they placed the naked bodies of their deceased out in the open on top of the towers, one for the men and one for the women, for vultures to come and feed on. The corpses would be arranged in a sitting position and a priest would stay with them to watch which eyeball was plucked out first by the scavenging birds. If it was the right eye, it signified luck for the deceased, if it was the left, it meant unrest in the afterlife.

We begin to climb to the top of the men's tower, over the rocks and up the dusty path. The hills feel abandoned, worn down by decades of neglect; there is nothing to signify the importance of their past. Their sole function now is to serve as a viewing point, a pleasure spot for local families from which to gaze over the tan-coloured suburbs and planted fields below. As we ascend I am grateful for the breeze, the warming rays of the sun, an enjoyment only slightly marred by my smart leather shoes.

Occasionally, we have to negotiate boulders or the track becomes steep, and Vahid stretches his hand out to me. I take it but I don't need it, surprised by the coldness of his palms. He runs out of breath long before I do.

Hoping to free him from the obligation to treat me with chivalry, I decide to tell him about my childhood. I used to climb trees in bare feet, I tell him. I was a tomboy until I was at least thirteen.

'A tomboy?'

'A girl who acts like a boy,' I explain. 'I used to catch spiders in a jar and pull the wings off insects. I once got into a fight with the biggest bully in school. Every day I came home muddy and covered in bruises. I used to hide from my mother to avoid taking baths.'

Vahid laughs out loud, which feels strangely rewarding, his rough, stubbly face becoming softer and less gruff. I can tell by his expression he wants me to continue; his pace has slowed and he is looking at me.

I tell him about the flat countryside where I grew up. The unpaved roads, the nearest neighbour a ten-minute bicycle ride away. It should have been lonely with almost no children near by, but our acre of land felt like the universe. Each day I remained outside from dawn to dusk, returning home only when my mother called me in for meals. I tell him my favourite pastime as a child was to pull crayfish from the algae in a neighbouring ditch, presenting the bounty to my father in a plastic pail. That it wasn't until years later I discovered he secretly flushed them down the toilet, breaking his promise to eat them for dinner. I describe the horrendously short haircuts my mother forced upon me, tired of combing knots from my hair. As a result, for years I was asked whether I was a boy or a girl. He looks at me, surprised, his brown eyes sympathetic, when I admit the relief I feel, even to this day, at being referred to as 'she' or 'her'; at the absence of any doubt that I am female.

Vahid studies me as if trying to imagine me twenty years ago, a boyish little girl with dirty knees and a collection of insects. He pauses, as if unsure whether to speak, a weariness settling over him.

'I was at the university of sciences in Esfahan,' he says wistfully. 'It is one of the most famous universities for engineering in the country. I lived in a dormitory, four guys to a room, and was captain of our football team. We travelled to universities across Iran for competitions and I wore a red armband over my uniform. Sometimes the crowd supporting the local team were so angry they threw bottles and cans at us when we walked onto the pitch.' He rolls up his sleeve, proudly showing me a scar where flying broken glass had cut deep into his elbow. 'I only came back to Yazd when my mom became sick. I was happy living away from home. She had cancer and went to the hospital for treatment so I transferred to the local university, to help my sister take care of her and my father.'

He describes visiting his mother, seeing her frail in

the hospital, her hair falling out in clumps after gruelling sessions of chemotherapy. No meals were provided, so patients were fed by their families, but his mother couldn't stomach the rice and cans of tuna fish he and his sister tried to cook. She lost nearly twenty pounds in the five weeks she was there, able to eat little more than dry biscuits and weak cups of tea. When she came home she was too weak to do anything but lie down. They made up a bed for her on the sofa. The only book she reached for was the Qur'an. Vahid describes how on occasion he helped to feed and bathe her. He describes the shame he'd felt helping her out of her clothes, seeing her thin and shivering in her underwear. By the following year she made a full recovery, but to him she is still fragile, still needing him to remain close by. It is why he moved home again after finishing military service instead of applying for jobs in Tehran. Her illness has formed a kind of trap around him, filling him with guilt, making it seem impossible to seek a life away from her.

The trail gives way to a flatter, well-trampled path and I realise we have reached the top of the hill. The summit is deserted. The stone boundary of the pit where the bodies were once laid has begun to collapse on one side from neglect. We take careful steps as we pass around it as if trying to avoid disturbing any remnants of its morbid history. We sit on the edge of the tower wall and a gentle wind dries our faces. The view around us is nondescript, even dull, but I find the combination of sheep, gnarled shrubs and multi-storey apartment buildings beautiful. I take some pictures of the scenery, the landscape, but none of Vahid, capturing instead the streets where he once learned to ride a bicycle, to drive a car; the city where I imagine he will spend the rest of his life.

'Can I ask you a question?' he asks, sounding shy, as if he's debated asking it for hours. 'How are you going to manage for one month in Iran without having sex? Won't you try to have sex with someone while you are here?'

For the first time I feel responsible, aware my answer will form a template for his thinking for years to come. I know his information is drawn from satellite television and Hollywood films, where characters fall into bed after the briefest of introductions.

I gently explain that sex isn't such a big deal, that I haven't had a boyfriend in over nine months. There are no such rules, nothing is so rigid or predictable. Sex in many ways chooses you, I tell him. Although I'm not sure myself what that really means.

I don't tell him what I've discovered as I get older: that when it comes to sex I practise a self-protective restraint: the quick peck on the cheek, the slipping downstairs to get a taxi, the lack of expectation or certainty on both sides. I keep from him the sad realisation of how quickly desire can dwindle, the gestures becoming empty, the initial charge often fading to nothing. I simply tell him such experiences were indeed plentiful, but they were also the most lonely of all. I know he doesn't understand what I am saying, can't imagine such a thing. I am no longer talking but thinking out loud. He waits for me to say more but I finish, slightly embarrassed at having said too much, at having answered questions he hasn't asked me.

'And what about you?' I ask.

'What about me?' he says.

'Have you ever done anything?'

His expression turns serious and he glances downwards. 'No. I kissed a girl once at a party, but I didn't love her.'

He talks about the girls he sometimes sees in the tea-houses and parks, describes the invisible barrier in being able to get to know them. How he wants to be able to meet a girl and talk to her first before going through the necessary steps of asking about her family and reputation. He tried once, he confesses, to approach a girl he used to see in the library. She gave him her number and they spoke on the phone a few times. They arranged to meet at the library and sit near each other, on one occasion feeling brave enough to step out for coffee. But she became frightened and found his advances too bold, he says, going to see a religious consultant who told her to sever all contact.

We take a different route to my hotel and as we pass a mosque Vahid resumes his lecturing, tour-guide mode. But for the first time, it feels comfortable to tease him, to roll my eyes at him, and he punches me mockingly in the shoulder. We come upon a butcher's shop where a tray of sheep's heads are being stacked in the window, and I find myself pausing to stop and stare.

'They are for making *kalleh pacheh*,' he says, noticing my interest. 'It is a soup made from sheep's heads and feet that we eat early in the mornings. It has a lot of fat, so we have it before going on long hikes in the mountains. It is really delicious.'

I am at once thrilled at the prospect of tasting such a thing and frustrated by the difficulties. I know it will be served in some cavernous, male-filled den, a place polite women avoid. I can't possibly think about going alone, not even as a foreigner.

Vahid looks at me, puzzled, then smiles, comprehension spreading across his face.

'I understand now!' he exclaims. 'You aren't interested in monuments or historical places. You are only interested in food! You came to Iran for its food!'

'Yes!' I say, with growing excitement, and he strikes his hand to his forehead in realisation.

'Aha! So I will plan the rest of your days in Yazd for you. We will have a food adventure!'

I can't believe my ears; it is too good to be true.

Looking pleased with himself at the prospect of being my new food ambassador, Vahid sketches out a plan for the following day. 'We will have to start early,' he says, 'at five in the morning to have *kalleh pacheh*, and then I will ask for the pastry shop you liked to show us how they make their baklava. And you mentioned you wanted to see the butcher that has camel meat.'

He scrawls a set of precise instructions in Farsi and hands me the piece of paper. 'I am going to meet you at five to start our day tomorrow. Give this to the taxi driver so he will know where to come to pick me up so we can get started.'

I take my instructions like an enthusiastic schoolchild and Vahid continues to walk me home.

We enter the low-ceilinged bazaar where the moon-light filters through milky, stained-glass panels in the ceiling, bathing everything in a warm, amber glow. The crammed shops selling cloth, metal wire and cooking pots are concealed now behind heavy metal doors; the vaulted stone passageway has emptied of the bustle of shoppers and the calls of hawkers. Except for the echo of our foot-steps down the connected alcoves, the bazaar is entirely silent. Our shadows snake along the walls and spill onto the cobbled floor.

'Would you like me to sing to you?' Vahid asks suddenly.

'Can you sing?'

'Yes, my friends say that I have a good voice.'

The request is so random it makes me laugh, too irre-sistible and strange for me to say no. I watch the long, exaggerated silhouette of my scarf looming across the pavement, rising and falling as I nod.

Vahid begins to sing a melody in Farsi, one of the old-fashioned, big-voiced songs one hears late at night in the kebab shops, where the men sing of women's eyes and nightingales, sleeplessness and longing.

It is the first time a man has ever sung to me, a fact that makes me blush. There is a subtle, unintended strain of romance to the gesture but, rather than feel awkward, we feed off the sensation we are doing something brave.

We reach the heavy wooden door of my hotel and stop, our feet shuffling along the dusty stone floors.

'Did you like my song?' Vahid asks.

'Yes, it was beautiful.'

'Bye,' he says abruptly, spinning around. 'I'll see you tomorrow.'

Chapter Six

My hair is still wet under my scarf when I tug open the creaking wooden doors to my attic bedroom. I am careful to keep the squeaking to a minimum as I jiggle the brass padlock back and forth. I imagine this is where servants once slept, shaken awake at all hours with demands for cool drinks or to fetch wood for fires. Its sloping ceiling forces me to duck each time I enter and I am able to stand tall only when alongside the pair of single beds where I sleep. It is probably the hotel's worst room but I like its isolated location, that no one ever wanders past. Mine is the only room this way. I sweep my own floors and make the bed each morning. No one checks on me to see how I am getting on.

None of the other guests seems to know it is here or that this is the way up to the roof. The nights I spend here are quiet and undisturbed, a contrast to the noise and expectations of Vahid's family's apartment, the constant fuss where nothing goes unnoticed. Even the appearance of new freckles across my nose sends Vahid's mother to break off a piece of aloe vera. Consequently when I return to my room at night my first instinct is to peel away my layers of clothing and strip down to my underwear, to stretch and sprawl lazily across the bed. After a day of my sitting stiffly erect on the floor, guarding the round necklines of my shirts from slipping and exposing more than my collarbone, the sensation of the bedspread beneath my bare legs, and only my thin, faded camisole covering my breasts and stomach, has become a private luxury.

I tiptoe down two flights of stone steps, careful to avoid brushing against the wall that leaves chalky, powdery deposits on my navy coat. I slip past the hotel's dormant kitchen where two large refrigerators hum and the oily light from a fluorescent tube casts shadows of its nightly catch of flies.

It is something new and exciting to find myself being secretive, in this place where my comings and goings feel watched. Until now the desk receptionists have always nodded approvingly when I return each evening to collect my key. I see them ticking a box on a sheet of paper that rests next to the phone, relieved I won't be creating any trouble.

I wonder what they might make of my waking at 4 a.m. and dialling Vahid's number, hanging up after one ring. Or the childlike anticipation I feel in waiting for him to call and do the same to confirm he too has woken early and all was going ahead as planned.

Placing my key on the reception desk, I imagine him a few kilometres away, stepping over his parents in the dark on the way to the kitchen to drink a glass of water, splashing a handful over his hair in an attempt to flatten it down. I picture his mother stirring slightly as he gargles and spits toothpaste into the sink. Clutching Vahid's note to my chest, I slide the heavy wooden bolt guarding the hotel's entrance to the side and slip out into the cool morning air.

The sky is still pitch black. For the first time since my arrival in Yazd the roads are nearly empty. The only light comes from the bakery where men in white rubber boots and aprons pull hot ovals of sesame-flecked *barbari* from the ovens, wrapping them loosely in paper and selling them to the handful of people waiting outside. Turning away, I find the alleyways welcoming, quieter than when they are packed during the day. I enjoy the cold dampness that emanates from the stone walls, the sound of my coat swishing against my jeans, the sensation of striding purposefully with somewhere important to go.

I step out into the bright lights of a main street and almost immediately a car pulls up alongside and honks. The driver looks to be no more than twenty-five. A grey jacket is draped over the passenger seat beside him, a satchel and flask rest in the space behind the gear shift. I suspect the car has been borrowed from his parents to earn the equivalent of ten or fifteen dollars in the few hours before he goes to work in a factory or office. I climb in and hand him my piece of paper. 'Uh huh,' he says, scanning it, pulling away from the curb.

I have no idea whether what I have shown him is simply an address or if the first sentence says something more elaborate, such as: 'Please take this girl to …' The driver's face gives nothing away. Yet I feel oddly at peace, as if I am part of a script that has already been written, being shuttled between places I can't find on a map, guided only by a piece of paper.

Vahid is waiting for me as he promised, nodding approvingly that his instructions have been followed to the letter. He calls out, 'Hi, Jenny,' but says little more to me, speaking instead to the driver, telling him where to take us next. He sits up front, looking pleased to be in charge of everything. We stop again at a busy roundabout where minibuses and taxis are jostling for passengers. The sound of them calling out is energising, the noise of the day's commerce coming to life. I climb out of the car and follow Vahid down a concrete stairway that leads to an underground passage.

'It's this way,' he says. 'I can smell the soup from here.'

As we pass under the fluorescent strip lighting, I breathe in the musty scent and the dank air that flows up around us, taking it all as a good sign. Though it serves little purpose other than to sell cigarettes to pedestrians traversing the busy roundabout overhead, to me this underground passageway instinctively seems perfect. The ground is littered with banana chewing-gum wrappers. The rusty pipes overhead leak fluid. Vahid quickens his step as if he knows what I am thinking. I can see he feels not the slightest embarrassment in bringing me here.

'So the way it works is this,' he explains. 'We order our soup, and then we choose which parts of the animal we want and he'll put them on a separate plate for us. We have a choice of brains, tongue, foot, or eyeballs.'

'Eyeballs!' I gasp aloud.

He pauses in front of a large window that drips with slow trails of condensation, looking as if he has forgotten something.

'Are you sure you want to go here?' He hesitates. 'My mom has sometimes come here to buy soup for home but she would never sit down and eat inside.'

I understand he is seeking reassurance as much for himself as for me, thinking I might feel singled out and exposed. In response I pull my scarf forwards and tuck away any loose strands of hair in a show of modesty, knowing if my presence causes any offence it is Vahid who will be made to explain.

The *tabaakhi* has no more than four tables. One is occupied by a group of men in starched shirts with stiff, leather satchels resting in a tidy row at their feet. Their collars are stuffed with overlapping sheets of Kleenex and they hunch forward over their steaming metal bowls to avoid splashing themselves. In between slurps they mop the perspiration from their foreheads with bunched-up handkerchiefs held tightly in their fists.

At first I am almost disappointed, having expected coarser, rougher company. The floor is swept clean instead of littered with spat-out bones and discarded bits of cartilage. Used paper napkins have been crumpled and placed in the bin. A turbaned mullah chants the morning prayers from a TV hung on a bracket on the wall, all long vowels and exaggerated rhythm. One of the men gets up from his chair and switches the channel, settling on a football match between Argentina and Brazil. Behind cupped hands the men discreetly scrape at their teeth with wooden toothpicks, impeccable manners I find disconcerting. Perhaps it is these same manners that allow me to be here at all, I remind myself. My presence is marked only by fleeting glances of recognition and shuffling of chairs.

A white-bearded man enters and breaks the silence, grumbling praises to Allah as a greeting to no one in particular. His long, baggy shirt and trousers could easily pass for pyjamas and the undone metal clasps on his sandals flap as he moves. He places a battered pot and lid brought from home on the counter, explaining his wife is pregnant with their fifth child and unable to prepare the morning meal without vomiting. '*Ya ali,*' he mutters through thick, dry lips, asking God to grant him strength. As soup is poured into his pot with scraps of the cheaper meat from the foot, he takes notice of us and turns, speaking solely to

Vahid. He assumes by my presence Vahid has plans to go abroad, tells him what a shame it is for Iran to lose her young people. 'The West isn't the same as here,' he says, 'they don't care for each other as we do in this country. You could die in the street there and no one will notice you,' he warns, shaking his head in a mournful fashion. Vahid nods respectfully as one might with a grandparent, as though humouring him but thinking him hopelessly old-fashioned. Vahid then turns, bringing the conversation swiftly to an end, ordering bowls of soup and a plate of tongue and brains for us to share.

The teenage boy behind the counter begins talking as he fetches two tin bowls from a shelf behind, as if nothing were unusual about our arrival. He notices my interest, my leaning to peer over the counter, and invites me to step into the rear to see where he works, looking bemused. He shows me the gas flame he uses to burn the hairs off the sheep's heads, the enormous pot he places them in to boil. He points to a cleaver he splits the feet in two with – a trick the previous owner taught him – to encourage the bone marrow and gelatine to spill out and thicken the broth. In spite of the streaks of grease on his white smock and the blistered skin on his fingers from pulling scalding meat from bones, I am shocked to learn the young boy is also the owner. With his chin, he gestures at a small platform bed tucked under the counter, where he sleeps from midnight until 4 a.m. while the heads and feet simmer with onions and turmeric. He once overslept while making the soup for a wedding, he says, waking to find it had reduced to little more than a dark, wobbling jelly. He smacks his lips, describing how he couldn't resist spreading a few spoonfuls on bread, before thinning it again with several teapots full of water.

Beside the counter a large bucket of discarded skulls and feet steam faintly, having been stripped clean of all meat and gristle. Vahid tugs on my sleeve impatiently, urging me to rejoin him. 'The leftover bones are always kept separate,' he says. 'Some men will come later to take them. They grind them to powder and use it for fertiliser.'

'Tell her it is because of the sanctions,' the boy tells Vahid, 'that before the revolution we could import everything.'

We are all too young to know anything of life before 1979 but I know it already as commonplace, to reminisce about the 'Shah times' when access to foreign commodities was easy. I've seen photos of the years when Tehran could have easily been mistaken for London or New York, with women dressing in miniskirts and Western goods lining the shelves. Days when it was not yet illegal for men to wear a tie and young graduates worked in the glassy office complexes of European firms in the expanding district of Abbas Abad. Tourists drank Martinis in the lobbies of the Intercontinental and the Hilton, and went to nightclubs to hear Ebi and Googoosh, who have since gone into exile. Wealthy Iranians apparently used to think nothing of flying to Paris to go shopping or to New York to visit their children studying for PhDs. Now they must pay hundreds of dollars for visas that take months and a mountain of documents to obtain.

In a flurry of gestures and excess, the boy passes a chipped oval plate of wobbly meat to Vahid, who taps his heart in a gesture of thanks. I can guess that the portion has been doubled as a show of kindness.

We take our seats in the corner and another boy drops a newspaper-wrapped parcel on our table. Vahid opens it to reveal a warm stack of bread and passes the boy a handful of notes. Our soup is fluorescent yellow from turmeric, and the tongue and brains are sprinkled with cinnamon and lemon juice. Our spoons slice through the meat easily and I am pleased to see that, like me, Vahid possesses a generous appetite in the morning. He passes me a parchment-like slab of flatbread, eager that I eat in the same fashion as he does. He instructs me to *tileet*, to tear the bread into bite-sized pieces and let them drop slowly into the broth. 'Wait,' he says, reaching across to push my bread fragments under the little pools of fat that glisten on the surface of my bowl. 'Now,' he nods when they have become engorged and fluffy, 'it's ready.' As we sip the soup from our spoons and pass each other more bread to scoop up what little broth remains in our bowls, Vahid begins to explain our plans for the day.

'I have asked about where the camel butcher is. We have to go to a place about thirty kilometres outside of the city. I will find a taxi and bargain the price to take us there.'

'A butcher thirty kilometres outside of the city?' I ask. 'Don't they have these kinds of places in Yazd?'

'No,' Vahid says, looking startled. 'It is very messy to kill a camel. We have to go to a special place for that and its location is outside of the town.'

I am confused at first and start to laugh. But soon I realise there has been a terrible misunderstanding. This wasn't what I'd meant at all. He is talking about taking me to a slaughterhouse.

'Are you serious?' I ask, stunned. 'Will they let us go there?'

'Yes, of course they will let us go there. Don't you want to go there?'

I turn the plastic shakers of sumac and lemon juice in my hands, unsure whether to feel pleased or hurt, whether he really thinks I am so morbid with such a taste for gore.

'Don't worry,' Vahid says, leaning forward, 'for us it is normal. When I was fourteen I helped my father kill a sheep in our back garden for the end of Ramazan.' I look at him. He hasn't shaved this morning and the thick stubble on his face and the deep creases in his forehead make him look older than twenty-five.

'OK, let's go,' I say, finally, wiping the soup from my chin and rising to wash my hands at the small sink in the corner. We leave a few crumpled ten-thousand-rial notes on the counter and I readjust my scarf before stepping outside into the cool morning air.

Vahid hails a taxi and from the gruffness of his voice I

can tell he is bargaining with the driver. 'I have agreed a good price for us,' he says and turns to open the back door for me. He makes to get in the passenger's seat next to the driver, but then pauses and shuffles across the back seat beside me. 'I will sit next to you,' he says, smiling, but looking shy.

The driver eyes us carefully in his rear-view mirror, hesitates, and then with a shrug of his shoulders raises the volume on his radio and pulls away from the curb. The traffic is just starting to build as we drive first east, then south through the city and towards the desert. I take my first photograph of us, sitting together in the back of the taxi with the sun behind us just beginning to rise.

Even from a distance the slaughterhouse is ugly and shabby, its construction little more than rough-painted breeze-blocks oozing a crumbling, cement paste. As we get closer I can see the surrounding acre of grey asphalt, parked with battered old Peugeots and dusty pick-up trucks. A group of men in bloodstained smocks lean against one wall, smoking cigarettes, speaking quietly into their mobile phones. Their bearded faces glow in shades of amber, lit by a single yellow light bulb hanging from a wire over the doorway.

One of the slaughtermen sees me and calls out loudly to Vahid, 'Isn't she scared to be here? Women don't come to this place.' I hear the word 'Canada' and feel a number of heads turn in my direction, causing my face to burn with embarrassment. I lower my gaze and concentrate instead on Vahid, the slightly uninterested tone of voice I am accustomed to, explaining me away in Persian.

We walk to the entrance and I peer through the doorway. The dozen men inside have the dark complexions of Kurds or Afghans, black eyes and sunken cheeks that seem suited to this place. Wearing high rubber boots and thick woollen caps, they lean against the cracked, tiled walls in sluggish expectation. Long knives with chipped plastic handles swing from the loops of their belts as they joke and gesture lazily.

A small pick-up truck reverses to a concrete loading ramp opposite. With a bang it drops its rear metal panel to unload a densely packed cargo of goats and sheep. Some of the animals sense danger and urinate without control onto the cracked, stained floor. Others bolt for the entrance and try to escape. I stifle an inane giggle as the men grab the animals by a leg, dragging them back limping on the other three. It is the kind of confused laughter that comes at a funeral or on hearing something shocking, usually accompanied by a feeling of helplessness and despair. I fear someone will demand an explanation for my presence or point a finger in my direction, assuming people normally come here to choose a carcass for a birthday feast or wedding. I can do little but stand and lean against a wall stupidly, fiddling with the ends of my scarf in a way I know must look furtive and self-conscious. I avoid their languid, showing-off smiles and the way they regard me, over their shoulders or out of the corners of their eyes. It's too late now to huddle into a corner and lower my gaze, to try to make a point of not being seen.

The killing is swift and methodical. As each animal's throat is cut it is laid on its side to bleed over a metal grate. Despite myself I am unable to take my eyes off the twitching carcasses, or the men who surround them in gangs of four. I step back as they roll their thick sweaters up to their elbows and take long final drags on their cigarettes, hoisting the bodies onto large metal hooks. In a matter of moments the animals are skinned and their organs removed, tangles of warm intestines and livers and hearts heaped into buckets without ceremony. It is only when the half-digested, grassy contents of their stomachs are emptied into a wheelbarrow that Vahid gags and rushes outside. I feel a flicker of irritation at him for suggesting we come here and then not being stoic enough to tolerate it.

Within moments the animals have been transformed into clean rows of pink bodies and the procedure calms to something routine and mechanical. It feels impossible not to soak it all up, the marked contrast to the prettiness and constrained order of how I live. In London I can be made to feel guilty taking even a pair of scissors to a bunch of parsley instead of plucking it leaf by leaf onto a sheet of paper towel, working in a state of such fierce concentration I have on occasion sliced straight through my finger or scorched a pattern of lines across my arm. I recall the hours I've deliberated over recipes for my classes, things I dream up and am dying to teach. The tiny quails I want to spear onto skewers and roast, the messy bowls of octopus braised in olive oil with whole hunks of potatoes, ideas that never see the light of day. Everything must be tempered and tamed for the people who come, wanting to know how packages of sauce could be doctored with this or that, who laugh, giddy at the heaviness of my knives in their hands. People who weekly cause me to wake in the middle of the night startled, grasping for imaginary ingredients around me: a bunch of carrots, a wet fish, anything I can improvise for a class at a moment's notice.

Vahid stumbles back inside, pressing a tissue clumsily to his mouth. He looks at me surrounded by all this blood and mess as though I am a delicate bird or newborn chick, fearful I am in danger of breaking down into tears. He inspects my face for signs of sadness or melancholy, but the truth is I am perfectly calm. I see the twitch of a smile and he shakes his head as if bemused by something. He paces a little as if to make it clear he has overcome his queasiness, his feet leaving a circuit of wet prints across the floor. He seems disconcerted by the lull in activity, by the sounds that have now died out, as if asking himself 'What now?' With visible excitement he shouts and points over my shoulder to the brick wall outside, where the heads of two camels are just skimming the top of the perimeter. He nudges me to go towards them but I've seen all I need to, obtained whatever self-validation I've supposedly come for. He insists, pushes closer at my elbow, urging me towards the doorway, and because we are here and because I've been so straight-faced it feels impossible to back out now. Annoyed at being caught up in this absurd game of chicken, I take a deep breath and allow myself to be pushed into the eerie silence looming outside. As I walk I feel unavoidably tender towards every part of my body, my hands crossing in front of my abdomen, the sound of my breathing loud in my ears.

A teenage boy leads the camels through the entrance, tugging heavily on their ropes, causing their fleshy muzzles to pull away sharply exposing their teeth. I wince at his smirk, which feels all for my benefit as he tethers the animals to the rusted bumper of an old Renault 5. The camels kneel down on the pavement, blinking their wet, brown eyes, their mouths pulled up in what could almost be a grin. They flare their nostrils and snort away the moths that flutter around them, and from where we stand I can smell their damp, malty breath. I have the urge to reach out and stroke their long, fuzzy necks. As I move forward Vahid leans in close beside me. 'Camels are very emotional creatures. They must be killed one at a time, separately, and it takes two men. If they see the knife, or the killing of the others, they become violent and it can be dangerous. They could sit on us or kick us and break all our bones. I have heard many stories of that.'

An older man comes out and unties the smaller camel, leading it brusquely into a small room at the back.

Instinctively the camel follows with its head bowed and its hind legs clip-clopping on the asphalt. Onto its hide someone has painted the Persian numerals for fifteen – the five in Farsi being shaped like a heart upside down.

'Come, Jenny,' says Vahid, turning on his heel to go back inside. Seeing my reluctance, he grabs my hand and breaks into a run. I am startled less by the schoolboy gesture than by his willingness to put us both in danger. We both know for a man to hold an unmarried woman's hand is both reckless and illegal. Instead of dropping it when we reach the entrance, he tightens his grip, forcing me to turn slightly towards him. I squeeze his hand in response, not sure whether I am encouraging him, but unable to bring myself to push him away. The metallic, protein smell of the room drains me of any need for interpretation. I simply feel grateful for being touched. Stepping over a drain and the coils of a long, rubber hose, we retreat until our backs press against a damp, bare wall. Vahid moves in to close the remaining space between us, his neck inches away from my nose. I find it comforting to detect the scent of the cologne, a generic male scent of musk and limes that he must have rubbed into his skin before coming to meet me that morning.

The camel is crouched in a small heap on the floor beside a pair of massive metal scales. In a far corner a dead cow lies slumped on a metal dolly, water trickling from a hose inserted into its mouth. The room is airless, the single entry door has been closed, and the whirring metal fan overhead creates little wind. Underneath my manteau, my jeans and cotton shirt cling heavily against my body. Two men approach the camel from opposite sides and it sniffs the air as if expecting the deposit of a cucumber or carrot into its leathery mouth. The older of the two yanks its yoke to turn its head violently in one direction while the other makes a deep, forever slash across its throat. Vahid pulls me back as a pool of crimson seeps across the floor towards us and I feel the rough tips of his fingers twitch in my hand.

I slouch with relief that it is finally over and the limbo fills with the noise of our exhaled breath. I try not to attach feelings to the smells nor mental words to the sounds, pushing it all aside for later. The door is thrown open suddenly and bangs on its hinges, and my heart sinks as the second, larger camel is brought in. The young boy who had first tied the camels up outside struts past us with a knife and begins to sharpen it with clumsy strokes.

'What's he doing?' I ask Vahid. 'Doesn't it need two men?'

'I don't know,' he whispers. 'Maybe he wants to kill by himself to show off in front of you.'

The camel kneels down in response to the sharp hisses, folding itself into a calm, tidy package. The boy looks to be making the most of the tension, circling the animal, his rubber boots squelching loudly in the blood. As he leans forward, his dark, oily hair falls into his eyes and for the first time I feel truly frightened. We are alone in this room with its stained floors and metal hooks, the three of us and the camel.

The boy aims for the camel's throat, but instead of the long, sweeping cut that is needed, he makes just a narrow, but deep, incision. The camel bolts upright in terror and runs towards the light of the entranceway, out into the parking lot. A number of older men standing outside their offices yell angrily as it races around in circles, spraying them with an uncontrolled jet of blood. The boy tries in vain to grab the camel's yoke, but it only becomes more agitated, galloping in a frightened and confused circuit, throwing plumes of grey dust into the air.

We step over abandoned weighing scales and kicked-over fragments of metal into the life-giving wind outside. The camel struggles for another few minutes until at last it stops to collapse on the pavement.

'*Mash'allah,*' says Vahid softly, releasing my hand.

The camel lies on its side, its papery, brown skin marked with blood and its limbs curled and motionless. We back away as the Kurdish boy advances, slicing stupidly at the gash in its throat, the gesture face-saving and pointless. Two men in plastic flip-flops begin hosing the blood from the pavement and it foams pink as it washes across the parking lot, into a gutter.

I find a patch of sunlight along the wall and lean against the bricks, wanting to extract some warmth through my layers of clothing. Vahid looks flushed and awkward, his brown eyes suddenly tired and ringed with circles. More camels are being led through the entrance, with more blue numbers painted onto their sides. A group of men approach and huddle together, talking in loud, urgent voices. Vahid turns and speaks to one of them, who replies with an absent shrug. They raise their hands and draw trajectories in the air, pointing from the camel to the back room of the slaughterhouse. One of them leaves briefly, returning with several lengths of rope.

Two large camels are brought over and harnessed to the legs of the dead animal, lengths of frayed rope are looped around their necks. The last thing I see as we walk back to our taxi is the sight of them, being whipped and pulling obediently, their cargo dragging, leaving a thick, wet trail behind.

From the subdued way he opens the door for me I can tell Vahid is keen to atone for the miscarriage the morning had become. We are let out at a crossroads I vaguely recognise, close to a pastry shop we'd stopped at a few days before to buy little metal boxes of pistachio and coconut baklava cut into tiny squares and sprinkled with rosewater. I have been eating them ever since. A few pieces popped into my mouth in the morning, a few more as I sit reading in the dim light at bedtime.

As we walk inside, I can smell honey, lemon and roasted almonds. The men working inside lift scorched trays of Yazdi cakes out of the oven. They stop, looking happy to see us, brushing flour off their hands and extending them to Vahid, clapping him on the back. Vahid seems glad to be interacting once more with men. The environment is mercifully innocent and carefree.

The kitchen is like a child's fairyland. Everywhere there are trays of tiny doughnuts ready to be rolled in icing sugar, miniature saffron biscuits flecked with cardamom and raisins, and clover-shaped cookies made from chick-pea flour. They turn to me and say the magic words: I wasn't to leave until I had tasted everything.

Hands and fingers appear from all directions, bearing trays of sweets, cookies and cakes. One is sticky, one is crumbly, one is covered in date syrup, while another has been rolled in sesame seeds. Stopping only to brush the crumbs and icing sugar from our laps and to lick our fingers, we taste and nibble until our stomachs ache. The owner of the factory, a middle-aged man with salt-and-pepper hair and a short, well-trimmed beard, brings out glasses of rosewater lemonade and asks Vahid whether we'd like to try making *pashmak*.

The *pashmak* machine resembles a giant metal tarantula. As it hums into action, its legs pick up the warm, fluffy strands of yarn spun from sugar and sesame as they come out of a central orb that melts the ingredients together. We collect the delicate, gauze-like fibres and weave them around our fingers, stopping only to place a fine thread into our mouths and feel it melt on our tongues, condensing into hard beads of sugar on our teeth.

When we finish we are surrounded by a pastel rainbow

of spools. Some of it is stuffed into sesame-flecked bread and offered around with glasses of tea. Most of it will be carted away to decorate cakes or to be sold for weddings. One of the men picks up a few strands of pink *pashmak* and winds it into a kind of necklace, lowering it over my head and smiling at me. I wash my hands at a small enamel sink in the corner and look in the mirror, thumbing my little sugar necklace and glancing at my reflection.

Behind me Vahid is speaking in the soft, deferential tone I've heard him use at home with his parents and uncles. His arms are crossed across his chest as he speaks. I understand the details of their conversation without explanation. I have begun to understand the changing textures of his voice, just as I have become accustomed to the varying natures of his face. At times he is just a shy boy whose life has been spent entirely separated from girls: at school, on buses, at the bakery where queues form – women to the left, men to the right – to buy stone-baked bread. Surrounded now by men with their wide, silver wedding bands, the jutting paunches of their well-fed stomachs and their temperaments softened by their wives and children, Vahid takes on the full stance of an adult, leaning slightly on one leg, slicing his hands through the air as he talks.

Vahid's status in life, his family name, his military service and lack of employment are all details to be shared, questioned and discussed among strangers. I feel sad as I watch the grains of his young life get threshed and picked over, its quiet details scrutinised and evaluated. To get a job he will need to show that he has been in the military, that he has no close family in the West and no interest in going abroad. To marry well he will need to have the right surname, then acquire the essentials of a job, a house and a car. Privacy is something kept for other matters – the difficulties within a marriage, sexual longings, the pale forearms of a wife or sister – but the facts and progress of his twenty-five years are public details, open to examination by all.

As we leave the pastry shop, the afternoon sun is high and the streets are shadowed and deserted. Yazd's families are indoors, whispering afternoon prayers or sitting around their *sofrehs*, eating lunches of stew and rice. We walk through the alleyways that run parallel to the main street where taxis still hum and the occasional bus thunders past.

Vahid walks quickly, his hands slightly clenched at his sides. His scowl has returned and his eyes seem troubled. I let him hurry ahead of me, his short noontime shadow floating at a sharp angle beside him, following him along the stone walls and spilling onto the rough, pot-holed ground. He appears to have forgotten me and it takes him several moments to notice he's left me behind. Finally, he stops and turns around, his expression tense.

'Why are you rushing? What is wrong with you?' I ask.

He takes a few careful steps towards me, breaking the silence with the crunching of pebbles and kicking up a small cloud of dust. I feel him studying me, unsure.

'Let me make a phone call here,' he says, gesturing to a green phone booth in the street. 'Just a moment, please. My cellphone is out of credit.'

I watch him dial a number and wait several moments. Eventually he hangs up without speaking.

His eyes betray an instant's hesitation. 'Let's go home. For lunch,' he says.

We walk to a bus stop and quickly become separated in a sea of black gowns, smoking men and well-behaved schoolchildren. The bus arrives and he boards at the front, while I join the rush of covered faces clambering in at the back. He cranes his neck to ensure I get on OK and I stand among the silent sway of women who hold firm the hands of their children. I allow myself to stare out the window and daydream, knowing Vahid will call out for me when it is time to descend.

Chapter Seven

It is nearly two but it feels like evening. Vahid climbs the staircase as if he has something important to do. From four steps behind I notice the loose stitch of the fake Adidas logo on his shoes, the embossed letters on the heels almost fully scuffed away. I feel a sense of homecoming as we pass the mats piled with loafers and rubber sandals, followed by relief when we arrive at his family's door. I am still parched from the excess of sugar I've eaten and craving the cold metallic taste of water from the tap.

Instead of ringing the doorbell as he always does, Vahid jangles a set of keys in his pocket. I recognise the significance of it immediately, but it doesn't occur to me to find it strange. If anything I'm glad for the chance to be left alone, spared his father's routine questioning about the price of a kilo of meat or a tankful of gas.

'My mom will be home soon,' Vahid says as if to reassure me, leaning against the wall for me to step inside first.

A linen cloth covers the bowl of fruit on the table. The teacups have all been washed and set in the drainer over the sink. For once the television has been switched off and we behave like a pair of schoolchildren set free. We throw our bags into a heap on the rug, draping our coats on the backs of chairs. Vahid goes to the kitchen to rummage for cups and glasses. It strikes me how nimbly he seems to flit between ages, how quickly he ages and grows young again. Outside this house his stubble seems darker, his face characterised by lines and determination. Back in his mother's kitchen, he could pass for a teenager. With his jacket removed, he is wearing a T-shirt with thin orange stripes from his shoulders to the ends of his short sleeves. It's a shirt I'm guessing his mother bought for him, still thinking of him as a little boy.

Vahid boils the kettle and sets bowls of dates and dried mulberries on a tray while I walk through the living room as if it were a museum. Emptied of people, it seems larger, the mementos covering every surface more careful and deliberate. *Nowruz* cards are tucked between vases of dusty, plastic flowers. Photographs nestle among stiff twists of lace. I pause, seeing them fully for the first time, Vahid and his sister's lives curated from infancy. In prints faded with age and sunlight, they perch in the arms of various relatives, their mother rarely straying outside the frame. Gradually they appear separate, both from their parents and from each other, exhibiting the courage and independence that come naturally with youth. Vahid stands poised to kick a football, grinning widely with a missing front tooth. His sister poses in a pale blue school uniform with a satchel of books, a matching headscarf secured with a knot under her chin. As the photographs track her passage through adolescence, her scarf becomes looser and bolder, darkening to shades of scarlet and purple. Eventually it is worn tossed across the left shoulder in the same style I wear mine. Soon after that she disappears.

I search for her among the remaining frames and pictures but she is conspicuously absent or out of view. On the rare occasion I am able to find her, she appears as a dot on a landscape, an abstract figure like a cloud or tree. It takes me a moment to see the pattern: that when she appears she is always flanked by Vahid's father or uncles, partially obscured. Sometimes only a shoulder or a part of her face is visible, the rest of her lost behind striped shirts and oiled heads of hair. It's as though efforts have been made to keep her from standing out, ensuring she stays deliberately tucked away.

I stand on my toes to grasp at a small pile of padded albums decorated with plastic jewels and glitter, placed up on a high shelf out of reach. The images inside startle me no less than if they'd spilled out and dropped onto the floor. There is Vahid's sister, again and again, one of a crowd of women surrounding brides in lavish white dresses. Her uncovered hair is set in stiff, shiny ringlets, her clothing covered in sequins and sparkles. In contrast to the photos on display where her hands are clasped modestly in front, she is bent forward, her bare arms dangling over another girl's shoulders. Her smile is broad and her mouth bright with lipstick, rings of heavy pencil circle her eyes, a look she copies many times. Made up, she could easily pass for ten years older.

They are the sort of photos I could imagine being circulated to a prospective suitor, upon reaching the mature stages of a *khaastegaari*; the spacing and symmetry of her features studied by countless relatives while deciding whether or not to proceed. I picture these same photos turned over and over in their hands, her face and body gradually plastered with critical thumbprints. Though I have never met her I can't help but feel sorry for her, envisaging her being picked over and judged.

At twenty-three, she is nearly a decade younger than I am, and I try to imagine what that must mean. To shelter and refuge within these boundaries of family and follow a path requiring total and unquestioning trust. I suspect she has never quarrelled with her parents as I have, never raised her voice to confront people pushing her on the Tube. That like Vahid she has been raised to fulfil a broad, collective expectation, to conclude her youth in a way that satisfies and pleases all.

I continue shuffling from one picture to the next, hungrily absorbing the details of the last two and a half decades. It reminds me I am merely a blip, with little or nothing to contribute. This is a home where Iranian lives are lived.

I reach for another photo that stands out from the others – a mottled black-and-white print under a sheet of glass. The mood is one of order and ceremony, a grand event taking place. The adults are wearing long, formal clothing. A cream-filled rolled sponge cake rests on a banquet table. Four boys are sitting upright on stiff, throne-like chairs, looking uncertain how to behave. The oldest boy is trying to smile for the benefit of the camera, but the others seem to chafe miserably under the attention. They are wearing white knee-length skirts, their row of uncovered knees shining and bare. By contrast the other children in the picture appear carefree and happy, their countless toys and dolls littering the floor.

'That is my father and uncles in Khuzestan,' Vahid calls out. 'It was taken at their *khatneh soori*. My grandmother waited until my father was five, then she took them all to the doctor together so they would be less scared. Thank God I was too young to remember my own operation. My mom asked them to do it when I was born.'

At first I think he is talking about the removal of tonsils or an appendix, but it soon becomes plain he is speaking of circumcision. My hands rise to cover my mouth in shock but the enthusiasm in his voice makes it impossible not to smile.

'Do you know what my grandmother did?' he says, encouraged by my expression. 'She asked the doctors to save their parts and she fed them to one of the chickens. Then she killed it and made my father and uncles eat it from the barbecue. It was the tradition and is supposed to bring good luck.'

The idea is so sweet and perverse it makes me shiver with laughter, pressing my hand to my stomach. It reminds me of the astonished giggles that accompanied my mother's explanations, when I was a child, of the phenomenon of a bruise or the mystery of a loose tooth. I remember how I used to listen to her in awe, tapping my fingers to my own body, bewitched by her assurances of its ability to heal or regrow. Though I don't belong in this house it kindles a similar affection, a claiming of its nostalgia for my own; just as I have claimed a regular place to eat and sleep on their carpet, their most prized possession, its rich pattern stretching plushly away under my bare feet.

Vahid's mouth is curled into a grin and he sets the tray he has prepared for us on a small table. He comes over to stand beside me, so close I half expect him to reach out.

He picks up another photograph that appears recent and hands it to me, of himself and his parents among a large group. They are sprawled shoeless on carpets in the shade of trees, the sun behind them fierce and unmarred by clouds. His parents look languid and relaxed in a way I have never seen them, their expressions uncomplicated and droll. The easy slouch of the people in the photograph suggests an atmosphere of being among family, who have seen everything and have no secrets.

The women are gathered in small circles, sisters and cousins who have coddled and breastfed each other's children, cooked one another's recipes for milk pudding and chicken salad. The men lean towards each other in heated conversation, hinting at the competition naturally existing between men. I imagine they must secretly appraise one another's cars, the beauty of their wives and the achievements of their children, yet can peacefully coexist on the holidays where they squash ten people into two cars to drive to Mashad or Bandar Abbas, all sleeping in two dormitory rooms, in each other's hair for days at a time.

Looking back at the photograph, I notice a platter of crisp heads of lettuce with two turquoise bowls resting on either side. A tall pitcher of gold-coloured syrup stands beside it, dappled sunlight glinting off the crystal handle. Vahid hooks his finger through mine, pulling my hand aside to look.

'Ah … a speciality of southern Iran. Its name in Persian is *sekanjabin*. It is a syrup made from cooking grape vinegar with sugar and mint. One of our neighbours even makes it with wild honey. My sister and I used to fight over it whenever my mom made it for us. I'm sure we used to make her crazy.

'My mom says the syrup is good for giving energy. She makes my father drink it with water and special black seeds. But mostly we dip lettuce in it and eat it with our fingers. It is so delicious you can't believe it. There is one farmer who is famous for the best lettuce in Yazd, all the women run to him when they see him. He comes to the parks with a donkey and sells from wooden buckets of ice. The lettuces are so fresh, water drips out when you cut them open. Between my father and me we can easily eat ten.'

His voice sounds tender and he leans in as if to touch me. Then he steps away and turns to face me instead. 'You see. Your place was empty,' he says, gesturing to the photograph, to a vacant patch on the blanket beside him.

At first I think he is talking to me like a sister; for all the days we have spent under the same roof. Perhaps by needing and seeking his protection, I have gone too far and stepped into her place. One evening a few days ago when his mother, too tired to cook, suggested we go out to buy kebabs, even I got swept up in it all. The spritzes of cologne and quick checks in the hallway mirror, the clambering to grab wallets and tie shoelaces. The same sense of ceremony I'd felt with my own parents and sister when going to the movies or the gas station for ice cream. I climbed into the back seat next to Vahid without thinking. Vahid's parents got into the front to drive. From a distance any stranger would have assumed we were a family, that his parents were my parents, that Vahid and I were siblings.

In the silence I hear the swishing of his jeans as he steps towards me. He is so close I can smell sweat and sheep wool on his clothes. I hold myself perfectly still as he approaches, as if any movement might encourage him or scare him away. He grabs my hands and his expression becomes tense. 'It's OK,' he says. 'It's safe here.'

I feel dizzy and nervous as he stares into my face. My body stiffens against the bookcase. He doesn't seem to realise how stern he looks, how inward and autonomous he still seems. He has needed no one in all the hours we've spent wandering the city, yet I realise I have been scraping at him for days. I feel excited now at having exposed some softness, yet apprehensive of bringing it to light. Carefully I squeeze his hands back as if he has put something fragile into my palm. Something I am scared of dropping. As if, if I'm not careful, I could ransack an entire life.

'Can I kiss you?'

I feel I'll go crazy if he touches or kisses me, though he has barely held or shaken my hand. I have all the vocabulary to reject him. I can do it quickly, even with tenderness. Tell him he is too young, too intact, too perfect to court me in such a way.

Vahid draws closer to me, still holding my hands. His first kiss is quick and unsure and he seems scared of disappointing me. He kisses me again, more earnestly and possessively, the pull of his arms becoming strong around my waist. His mouth tastes pleasantly warm and sweet, and the stubble on his cheeks grazes my skin. His clasp moves up to my ribcage, pressing into my body as if laying claim to me, telling me, 'You are mine.'

I can sense how vulnerable and unsure he is. His neck stiffens under my hand. I let it rest there a moment to try to reassure him and the tremor in his bottom lip suggests

116

he is giving in to his body for the first time. Instinctively I pass my fingers through his hair and the texture startles me. It feels unpleasantly coarse, like wires. His breathing quickens, becoming hot and aggressive on my skin, and I panic and push him away.

Vahid recoils, looking alarmed. Then tilts his head downwards as if I've struck him in the face. 'I don't know why I was kissing you,' he says, his voice rising shakily.

I look at his flashing brown eyes, his angry scowl, his arms crossed defensively across his chest: the strange combination of everything that is exciting about him and everything that drives me away.

'I think you wanted to kiss me because you like me,' I say quietly.

'No, I don't like you!' he shouts, backing away. 'I don't like you. I feel pain in my chest and I want to be free of this!'

Vahid lowers himself against the wall opposite, resting the weight of his body on his crossed ankles. The tea he has made has grown cold now. The unused cups are still stacked.

'Maybe I should leave you alone for a while.'

'No, come and sit beside me,' he says softly. 'Don't leave.'

I cross the room and crouch next to him. He takes my hand and holds it to his chest.

'I can't breathe and my heart is pounding,' he says in a low, quiet voice. 'What is happening to me?'

I feel almost chivalrous to see him like this. I want to

touch his face and put a hand to his cheek. In spite of the dormant calm I've acquired towards men, piled up instincts of hesitation and reluctance, I want to do something, to somehow reach out.

'It's OK,' I say, leaning across to stroke his hair.

'No! It's not OK!' he lashes out. 'You are mediocre. You aren't ugly, but you aren't beautiful. Other than your hair you have no nice features. I don't like you!'

I stand up slowly, my cheeks flushing crimson. I want nothing more than to get out of this room.

'You need to be left alone.' My voice comes out more dismissively than I intend and I begin moving around the room to gather my things.

'Don't leave me. Please come back. Come back and sit with me.'

'No,' I say firmly, leaning against the wall opposite. 'You come. You come to me.'

He stands up and looks at me puzzled. 'Jenny, I'm sorry. Please come and be close to me.'

I watch as he walks slowly towards me. He takes my hand and raises it to his mouth.

I can feel his hand is trembling slightly as he begins to pull me towards him.

Turning off the lights shouldn't have made it so dark. It is late April and the middle of the day. It is clear he has partially prepared for this, to approach me in this way. He leads me to the bedroom, his expression both calm and reckless. He pushes me down onto the bed. He climbs on top of me roughly, as if wanting to get it over with, never once looking at my face.

His hands on me feel rough and aggressive; he grasps at my breasts and scratches at buttons and clasps. For a moment I think he might try to force himself on me, but I manage to push him away.

'I want to see your body,' he says. 'You are leaving soon and I don't want to miss you. I don't want to miss you. You are perfect for me. I want you to be mine.'

His face is full of anguish and his hands move again around my waist. I am tempted to lie still when he reaches to unzip my jeans a second time. But to sleep with him would be only about his virginity, and I couldn't take such a memory or leave behind such a powerful imprint.

I push him off a second time and he slides onto his back, beside me. His eyes are closed, his expression limp and defeated. I want to do something for him, make some sort of gesture. I care for him and it shouldn't end like this.

Everything feels slow as if I am moving through wet fog. I reach inside the folds of his trousers and his breath quickens as he turns towards me. I press my cheek to his and feel his warm forehead against my face. '*Joonam,*' he whispers as I close my fingers around him. As his breathing quickens and his body tenses, he twists the ends of my shirt into a knot in his fist.

'Are you OK?' he asks again and again, his eyes wide and full of concern. He reaches for a cloth to wipe the stickiness from my fingers, more worried for my propriety than for himself, lying in damp clothing with his zipper still undone.

Rather than feeling embarrassed or shy, he offers me a place on his chest to lay my head. Quietly he whispers, '*Joonam, azizam,*' stroking his fingers through my hair. He seems grateful for the kindness I have shown him, as if I might just as easily have humiliated him instead.

Later at dinner Vahid takes the place next to me on the floor, a family of four sitting around the tablecloth. As usual the news is on the TV as we eat, our heads bowed, reaching for bowls and plates. I've grown accustomed to the relative quiet at mealtimes when it is just the four of us, Vahid's parents wasting little time on ceremony. Without a household of uncles and cousins, conversation is kept to a minimum and meals are not long, drawn-out affairs. Compared to the many hours of braising and frying, and the elaborate decoration, that go into preparing our meals, the act of sitting and eating is brief and perfunctory.

As his parents eat with their eyes glued to the screen, Vahid behaves with a new attentiveness that causes me to blush. He tugs out the best pieces of chicken for me. When my plate becomes empty he refills it with rice. In return I top up his glass of lemon juice, and pass him handfuls of chives and mint. We tend to each other with the affection of an old married couple, anticipating each other's needs. I look up at the faces of his parents, convinced they must guess or be aware of something, but they simply eat and watch television, staring in self-absorbed silence.

After dinner Vahid calls me to the window, holding open the blinds for me to see out between two slats. I press my nose to the dark-tinted glass to find that a dust storm has fallen upon Yazd, cloaking the city in a chalky mist.

'I will tell my parents that I am going to take you back now,' he says, 'but I want to walk a while together. I need to be alone with you.'

We step outside and as we walk swirling plumes of fine sand dance around us. I feel the fluffy particles collect on my hair, as pleasant as warm snowflakes on my nose and cheeks. We pass through the shadows of a line of cypress trees and Vahid stops.

'Close your eyes,' he whispers. I close them and feel his warm breath blow the dust from my eyelashes. I reopen them to see him smiling at me.

We resume our late-evening ritual of walking through the backstreets of the city which often takes place during the evening *azoon*. From the position of his parent's house we are closest to the minaret where it always begins, the first solitary call to prayer ringing out. At first I found it sinister and intimidating, but now I crave it. I like the formal recognition of the day changing into night, the voices adding their strength one by one to create a dense, overlapping sound. We listen as we pass down a narrow alley, the path clear despite the dust and fog. The sun has all but vanished and a few blurry stars are emerging in the sky.

'Jenny?' Vahid asks, looking down.

'Yes?' I murmur, still listening as the last notes of the *azoon* fade away.

'What do you think of me?'

The sensible thing would be to brush off his question. This doesn't feel like a conversation for now. Part of me is frustrated that he can't see this, but his face is so serious I want to tell him the truth.

In a shy, muddled way I have grown fond of him, and the strange way we have been thrown together. He is the last person I think of when I go to sleep. The first person I am curious about when I wake up each morning.

I feel pride that such a difficult person could single me out and treat me with affection. I have come to appreciate the way he glances over at me, keeping me constantly at his side. In return I feel protective towards him: how tired he seems, the default grimace he wears each day.

Beyond that, I can't understand what he might see in me, other than the draw one might expect from a lifetime without girls and sex. If we met in London we would have little cause to know one another. I can't imagine he would like how I live. My concrete walls and ceilings he would find cold and sterile. He would hate the oversized wooden table and taking meals from separate plates while sitting several feet apart. He would get restless and bored without the constant stream of friends and relatives ringing the doorbell. Probably he would frown at the absence of mementos and knick-knacks, at the single, bare light bulbs illuminating each room.

Perhaps now because we are equally alone, we seek each other out as we wouldn't elsewhere. But I know in a few days I'll leave Yazd and we won't see one another again.

We come to the end of the quiet laneway and I feel the impatient tug of his hand on my sleeve. I know he wants an answer to his question, to hear a profession, to kiss me again.

We step out into the bright lights of a wide avenue and by instinct we move apart and lower our voices. In the distance I see a car approaching, the full glare from its beams blinding in our faces. As it passes I have the feeling I should look down, yet I'm unable to turn my head away. I can just make out the silhouettes of four men through the darkened windows.

The car lurches violently and there is a squealing of brakes as it stops in the middle of the near-empty street. My heart goes cold as I watch it make a sharp U-turn and pull up onto the sidewalk beside us.

The front doors are thrown open and two men climb out, their heavy leather boots stomping the pavement. Revolvers and clubs hang from their wide, leather belts. Tidy rows of gold stars decorate the shoulders of their dark green uniforms.

One of the men looks at me closely and begins to shout at Vahid, a torrent of accusations and pointed jabs in the air.

Calmly, Vahid reaches into his pocket, handing over papers to the officer who has been shouting – his identity card and release papers from the military. The officer scans through the documents impatiently, scratching at the laminated plastic coatings with his thumbnail.

The officer turns and looks me up and down. But my coat is long enough, my scarf intact. I keep my gaze on the ground this time, fearing if I look up he'll read my mind and understand how inane this all seems. He passes the papers back to Vahid and I can see from their interaction it's a scene that has played out many times before, requiring certain lines; the script always the same.

The officer barks orders to the two policemen still seated in the car to get out. Then he turns, gestures violently at us to take their places. I turn and look to Vahid for guidance and see a shadow of agitation clouding his face.

'Call your parents and tell them to come and meet you at the police station,' the officer sneers. 'They can explain to us what you are doing alone with this foreign girl.'

'I am not calling anyone,' Vahid replies firmly, stepping forward to put his hand on the officer's shoulder. 'My phone is out of batteries. And my parents will be very upset to hear that you have frightened my cousin from London who is our guest.'

The policemen look around as if hoping for a crowd

to witness our humiliation, but the streets are empty, there is no one around. The only observers are in passing cars, slowing down and craning their necks out the windows. I can't tell whose side they are rooting for, or whether they are just grateful for the spectacle, for fresh gossip to share.

We stand on the pavement, their shadows looming over us, the effect emphasising that we are at the mercy of their mood. Vahid turns to me calmly. 'Jenny, do you have your passport with you?'

I reach into my bag and open my passport to the page where my visa had been stamped. He passes it to the officer who thumbs through it with excessive interest. He seems to be around forty, sporting the mandatory stubble. He leans towards me, glancing up from my photograph to my face, but instead of saying a word he just pauses and waits.

I continue to gaze down at my shoes. I have no idea whether he can read a word of English, or has the vaguest idea what any of the stamps mean. His expression softens slightly as he examines each page, squinting under the dim street lighting.

'Ask her how the police would behave in her country,' he asks Vahid sharply, motioning to me.

'My cousin is free in her country,' he replies, looking directly into the officer's face.

The officer smirks and hands my passport back to Vahid. '*Bashe*,' he says. 'Let it be.' They shake hands before the policemen climb into the car and drive away, vanishing just as quickly as they'd arrived.

Vahid turns to me and smiles. 'You really are my lucky coin. That was the first time I have avoided going to the police station.' He checks me over for signs of amusement, perplexed by my expression of deep concentration. He places his arm on my shoulder, gently repeating, 'Don't worry. It's all OK.' But it is my first taste of such mindless, random authority and I am lost as to what it must be like to live in such a way. I am half flattered the police should find me of any interest, annoyed they would bother with me at all. The facts of the moment, both comic and terrifying, haunt and reassure me at the same time.

Vahid leaves me to go into a cave-like store where oranges and lemons spill out of boxes, and bananas are piled on wide silver trays. He points to something and reaches for his wallet, but the vendor shakes his head as if we are toxic from our encounter with the police, raising his out-turned palm to his chest. Vahid points outside at me, calmly insistent, finally returning with two chunks of watermelon.

'I chose for you the part we love best in Iran,' he says. 'It is the centre that is the sweetest and has the fewest seeds. We call it the flower of the watermelon. I thought it would make you happy again.'

As we continue to walk a new silence falls over us. Awkwardness has gone and solidarity has risen up in its place.

'How *porru* we are!' Vahid laughs, a Persian word that literally means 'full of face'.

We eat our watermelon with savage vigour, falling into step, the juice beginning to drip through our fingers. Vahid pauses to spit the seeds delicately into a cupped fist, then holds out his hand for me to do the same. The combination makes me feel sentimental, almost more so than the early physical moment we shared.

It is well after midnight when we enter the labyrinth of the old city, the walls so narrow we must walk in single file. Behind me I can hear Vahid's breathing and the sound of his clothes scraping lightly along the packed mud and clay. I listen for other traces of noise, craving his touch, his hand rising to the back of my hair.

Chapter Eight

T he days after our encounter with the police are filled with anticipation. On the surface little seems to have changed. He waits for me with the same grimace and slackened posture and we walk through the courtyard without touching. He labours through the rituals of politeness with neighbours, nodding and kissing the hands of their children, shaking his head at the price of bread and milk. Finally we are released to make our way towards the staircase where our footsteps grind fresh desert sand into the concrete. It is there, in the pools of sunlight lying scattered on the floor, that he stops mid-step, one of his calves extended as if in a game of freeze. He listens for noise and, hearing none, he reaches for me and pulls me to him.

Each morning his kisses are hurried and shy, as if he is fearful my feelings for him may have cooled overnight. He kisses my hand first and the insides of my wrist, drawing back my sleeve to expose my veins. I sense it would feel inappropriate for him to kiss me on the lips without these first gestures of affection, had among the shoes of neighbours and the smells of their cooking. He is careful to avoid exposing my head, passing his hand carefully under my scarf to touch my hair underneath. He allows himself to graze the top of my neck with his fingers, knowing it will draw me closer. When he leans towards me, there is just enough light to make out his face before we lose ourselves in a fleeting forgetfulness. For a second we are just a boy kissing a girl, nothing wrong or dishonest, nothing treacherous, nothing to be ashamed of.

From that instant we become outsiders, even thieves, the familiar territory of his apartment block turning hostile. What we seek isn't jewels or money but the elusive possibility of having space and time. The narrow gap between our hands as we pour each other tea, the tiny void between our knees as we sit side by side: I can spend whole minutes, even hours staring at them and willing them away. I smell opportunity in the creaking of doors and the closing of windows, the clacking of the beaded curtain that on warm afternoons sways gently with the gust from the fans. All in the hope of a few moments of privacy, to be alone.

Our ritual, though only days old, forces me to trust him. Though I make no comment and betray no reaction to him, I know he is alert to the same opportunities and in search of the shortest path to me. I learn to cherish the few times in the day we'll speak or address each other directly, conscious of the barriers that keep us apart, the persistent presence of a chaperone. Some mornings we hardly talk at all, like two polite strangers, but I am sensitive to every time he passes near. I detect every subtle glance or motion in my direction, every hurried seeking and reluctant retreat. Sometimes we subsist a whole day on that first kiss, a rich morsel to chew slowly and draw out.

It makes me feel shy, remembering how I'd been at the beginning, embarrassed at how little I'd understood. I'd sat always on the most comfortable chair, failing to rise when elders came into the room, accepting shamefully expensive sweets purchased for my benefit and set out on silver trays. I'd basked in the false glow of foreign celebrity, wearing my scarf as if it were a game. But the longer I stay and the more I begin to comprehend, the more strange the idea becomes of leaving Yazd, the more unnatural the idea of going back to my empty home that is too big for me, to the spartan rooms and closets filled with denim miniskirts, and pink and green T-shirts, and rubber flip-flops, to life resuming its normal routine of tying aprons around my waist, of all the tasks of carrying and hauling and organising and planning. To a time where I'll glance again at the calendar hanging next to my desk in the hallway, safely counting down the days to the next trip, when I might close the windows and bleach out the fridge and abandon my home once more, occasionally looking back to recall something as rare and perfect as standing in a dark stairwell, with a boy's hand quickly passing through my hair.

How could I leave Yazd now when it is my job to peel the thick skin from the broad beans, a task his mother's hands, ravaged by chemotherapy, can no longer do? When it is only my arms that can reach the battered copper pot needed for boiling wild marigolds with sugar to make the syrup that will soothe sore throats this winter? When only yesterday I learned where the toolbox is kept, and which screwdriver to pass to his father when the plastic cover needs changing on the grumbling fan that hangs over the bathroom?

Even the sound of my name on their lips, spoken in the present tense and the possessive case – Jennifere, Jennifero, Jenniferemun – resonates through their third-floor apartment in a way that confirms my place here. So much so it seems almost natural when Vahid turns to me to say, 'Jenny, it's time.'

Separated by the polite distance of a green table, we easily could be strangers, counting our change and settling down for a treat. The bazaar is loud, even from the refuge of this archway, with the shouting of prices and the hammering of copper.

'I know it's a big risk but I want to take it,' he says. 'I have been observing you. I have seen you with my family and my friends. I watched how you behave. I want you to be my first love.'

131

Our rice-flour dumplings catch in my throat, the deep crimson syrup suddenly too dense to swallow.

For days I have wanted this, studied him too, dreamed of his hands on my body, knowing me in such a way. I've imagined myself the subject of the precise, painstaking attention he imparts to the routines that punctuate his day, the judicious lathering of his hands at the kitchen sink, the careful whispering of *salaat* before pressing his forehead to the ground.

In this inhospitable place where everything is overseen and decided, something delicate now seeks light and water to grow. But as I look out at the clamouring crowds drifting past, the vague swirls of black- and brown-draped limbs clutching shopping bags and children, my heart sinks at what I have known all along.

It isn't that what he is suggesting is dangerous or illegal, or that we would both be arrested if caught. I would be putting him in a position he would struggle to accept, shattering the truths of how he was raised. Vahid had always assumed he would be the first for a woman; no other possibility could have entered his mind. He had been taught to expect her to be as innocent as he was, that he would 'open' her for himself, a single discovery, a claim.

Whether I accept his notions or think them old-fashioned, anything we might do would be new for him alone. He would be navigating in the shadows of things that had already happened, of touches and caresses that had come in the past. I'm afraid it would be cruel to mark him in such a way, and I am fearful of being marked in such a way by him too.

The silence between us is tender and strange. I feel the sleeve of my coat soaking into a pool of melted ice on the table. But I don't move it. I don't say anything. I don't know what to say.

'You don't have to talk,' he says. His calmness unnerves me. How had I washed up into this new life where everything I did was marked and noticed, where everyone seemed to be reaching in and pulling something out of me?

For a moment I feel an overwhelming sense of missing him, missing even my self as I was at a younger age. I think back to how I'd felt slighted by the Irish boy who first slept with me, how my first relationship had troubled me in many ways. It had been his past that had hurt me the most, the knowledge that he had lost his virginity in a way I'd found crass. He'd been drunk and locked out of the house with a girl at a party, he'd told me, laughing. They'd had sex in a toolshed after he'd urinated among some rose bushes. Later, when I'd become more clear-headed, I'd quietly condemned the whole episode, always wishing I'd held on for something better, regarding it as something of a mistake.

I watch Vahid kick at the wide drain in the centre of the floor with the toe of his shoe. Though serious, he seems unburdened by any such concerns. Perhaps the fleeting nature of our romance has wiped these questions from his mind. Maybe it is better that way.

'I am leaving in two days,' is all I can bring myself to say. The words carry a finality that claws at my stomach. 'To do this now would only make things more complicated.'

'But I want this complexity,' he says. 'I want to take its risk.'

I turn briefly to look at him and shake my head. The folding metal chair Vahid is sitting on scrapes the floor as he leans in towards me.

'I had strong beliefs, Jenny,' he says, reaching for my hand. 'I wanted to have sex only with my wife. But you are something different for me. I am feeling the taste of love for the first time in my life and I don't want it to stop. I know you are leaving and I won't see you again. But I don't want to lose you. I want to have its memory.'

I take another spoonful of *faloodeh* and hold the icy mixture against the roof of my mouth. The cold creates a sharp pain that slides down my throat as I swallow. Even without looking across the table, I know my refusal must be hurting him.

The stall owner stirs the contents of a copper tub. He mutters orders to his helper, a young boy, to fetch his rose-patterned dishes from where they have been left by other customers in the neighbouring corridors. His back is to us, partly shielding us from view as he arranges his small display of plastic tubs of sugar syrup and blocks of sweetened sesame paste.

We continue eating without speaking. Our spoons clink against our bowls. As much as I appreciate Vahid and feel drawn to him, we aren't equals in any way. He is a twenty-five-year-old Muslim living in a country where you can be arrested for holding hands. I can't let myself consider him, or hope for something that is unchangeable.

He looks at my troubled expression, sees the difficulty I have in speaking. His brown eyes search my face and he releases my hand.

'Jenny,' he says softly. 'Do you know what you are to me, Jenny? You are *ba namak*.'

'What is *ba namak*?'

'It is a Persian word. It is a kind of saltiness. When food is *ba namak*, it means it is seasoned perfectly to our taste. To the next person it may be too salty. To another it may need more salt. But to this person, the food is seasoned exactly to be the most delicious just for them. You are *ba namak* for me, Jenny. Everything about your character – your confidence, your nice temper and all your experiences. They make you the perfect girl for me. Just for me.'

I turn to look at him, his eyes glowing with hope, his words so simple and uncomplicated. It gives me a start to remember how cold I'd felt when I first saw him, while feeling such affection towards him now. Ten days ago he'd written down his name and address for me, this gruff boy I'd been convinced I would never call or see again. He is now seeking more from me, asking for a permanent memory, a piece of me to keep.

I feel tears welling up and I brush them away quickly. He reaches again for my hand. This time his grip is strong and reassuring, anchoring me and pulling me in.

I gaze past him to see our reflections in a mirror on the wall, suspended over a basin in the corner. Vahid's head is tilted slightly in my direction, our faces framed by the stark white tiles. In this first, formal presentation of how we appear to the world, we are opposites in every way. His hair is black, my eyes are green; his tanned arms contrast with my pale hands and face. Yet I'm startled to find we look handsome together, even striking, rather than boldly out of place. The age difference between us appears diminished, the disparities have dwindled away. If anything, I seem like the one who is innocent, and Vahid the one who is taking the lead.

Vahid knows a pharmacy on the way home. He parks opposite and leaves me in the car. Even at nine in the evening it is packed with customers and a long line trails out the door. From where I am sitting I can see people rolling up their sleeves to analyse each other's skin ailments and rashes, discussing the nature and reason for their coughs. Vahid has disappeared into the swarm of figures crowding the counter where girls are dispensing everything from expensive bottles of L'Oréal shampoo to penicillin powder in paper envelopes. When he returns to the car he looks red-faced and embarrassed, and he sighs loudly in relief.

He removes an orange box from his bag. I lift it up to read the gold lettering printed on the front: *Rocket Love Rubbers. Made in Malaysia*. There is a drawing of a large penis-shaped balloon with jet flames underneath. I can't help but laugh, which makes Vahid laugh too. The image is such a stark contrast to our chaste, sexless surroundings. Vahid blushes slightly, placing his hand on my shoulder, the garish-coloured box a bizarre symbol of what we are planning to do.

He drives me home and we pass through the darkened streets in silence. The radio is switched off and the car hums loudly as the gear shift is moved from one position to the next. Vahid drums his fingers on the steering wheel as he drives, returning his hands to it each time he slots the lever into place.

'I had expected you to be skinnier, and your breasts to be larger,' he says suddenly. 'I couldn't stand to look at you the other day in my room. When I felt with my hand how hairy you were between your legs, I was shocked at how dirty you were.'

He says these things without ceremony, as if talking about the weather or football. For the first time a cheapness has crept into his voice. I stare at him, numb, and I feel myself stiffen. Without saying it to me directly, he is letting me know: I am something less to him and we are not equal in his mind either.

I am grateful to him for reminding me what this will and won't be. For putting this distance between us and maintaining this wall. He has done it for me, made my decision, enabled me to take something crucial from him. Our final night together will be a mutually beneficial swap: he'll feel like a man and I'll get a dangerous thrill. Perhaps he may look back and remember me fondly, in the only future he is destined for. Ten years from now with a soft-spoken wife beside him and two or three children, our one single night will flicker back into his mind. Even the short time I've spent in this country has taught me a few things.

His words continue to ring in my ears as he drives me home, steadying and putting me on edge at the same time. I shy away from him when it comes time to say good-night, mildly irritated when he pauses and listens for a chance to lean in. As he retreats to the car I catch myself wandering along suspicious, self-preserving fault-lines, thinking maybe he has done all this before. Wondering whether he is an expert at seeking out opportune moments to kiss girls, or if his talent is just a side-effect of living in Iran.

I wait until he is out of sight and slip out once more into the darkness, heading through the empty bazaar. My mind has filled with unanswered questions, things I want to understand. I find the internet café I usually go to. At this late hour there are only a handful of boys wearing headsets, playing video games, shouting loudly and shooting with large, wired-in toy guns. It makes it easy to choose a desk in the corner, one that isn't overlooked.

I don't know what I am hoping to find or even if it has anything to do with me. But I wonder what the consequences might be. I have no idea whether what we are planning is common or whether it has ever happened before, or if we would be in trouble if we were caught. The notion of punishment for unmarried sex is unimaginable to me but I know it has happened sometime, somewhere. In this nation of honour and obedience, surveillance and rules, the danger-versus-freedom debate is an unsolvable mystery. Maybe because in my case the foreigner is the female, Vahid would simply be patted on the back and chided for a slip-up in taste.

On my previous visit a student had leaned over and shown me a secret address that allowed me to bypass Iran's restrictions and access the *New York Times* and the BBC. I pull my chair close to the monitor and begin typing, unsure whether I will find what I am looking for. But there are videos upon videos and countless images, terrible things I'd only read about. I see men, women, boys as young as twelve or thirteen, all sentenced to death for breaking Iranian law. Their wrists are tied together behind their backs, nooses arranged and fitted in place. Crowds of people gather in circles around them, even children, some holding ice creams, many filming on mobile phones. Cranes pull them slowly up and away from the ground while the mob jeers and cries out that God is great.

Most go quietly, their faces numb, lifeless already when they are made to stand in the dirt. Some young men wave rebelliously and smile when the cloth sack is pulled from their heads, shouting curses and encouraging their relatives to chant. One woman is wearing a long, dusty chador, her only discernible feature the running shoes on her feet. She closes her eyes while five men fuss around her, calling out, '*Tamaam e,*' to indicate she is ready. Even as the crane has begun to lift, they step forward, tightening and adjusting the noose around her neck. When her feet leave the earth they begin to run and flap, those shoes desperately reaching out for solid terrain.

My hands tremble and I slide them under my knees, lowering my head in shame at what I've seen. I wonder if Vahid has ever watched such a thing, ever gone to witness such an awful scene. I try to imagine him pushing his way to the front of the crowd or jostling to get a good view. But I know he would find such a thing as wretched as I do, a fact that comforts me as I wipe the tears from my cheeks.

I turn back, ready to switch off my screen, and spot something I'd only vaguely noticed before. A group of policemen standing stiffly in a ring, while feet dangle limply over their heads. They are wearing the same dark green uniforms I'd learned to dread, the same brusque confidence on their faces. I shudder to remember the men who'd stopped and harassed us a few evenings ago, whose anger and smirking had made us feel so small.

Three more times the police have stopped us since, once even appearing out of the shrubs in a park. Each time Vahid and I were pulled up, separated, made to stand at a distance, while they went through their routine. We waited, frustrated and gawked at, itching to move on, for twenty minutes or longer, while they phoned in the details of Vahid's ID card and address, but rather than putting more fear into us, it lost a fraction of its meaning each time. By now I'd come to regard them as a nuisance. The last time I'd felt a surge of courage and refused to leave Vahid's side. We'd turned our backs on them as they mumbled their warnings, chastising us for the offence we'd caused.

I do not want to be quiet and obedient. I don't want to behave in a measured way.

I stand up from my chair, stumbling over a tangle of wires, and hastily smooth my scarf into place. At first the stale-smelling room with the green-hued posters of Khomeini on the walls and the sounds of boys shooting guns, is disorienting. But as I walk back to my hotel, the breeze composes me, ruffling the spiderwebs that flap overhead. I feel lucid again, grounded by the familiarity of the path.

It was not that we wanted to use my room. My room was the worst, most foolish choice. We had meant to go to a spot Vahid knew in the country, a tiny house near the mountains in Taft. The building itself was largely a wreck, he had warned, scarcely more than bare stones and a crude, slatted roof. From the well in the garden you could draw icy-cold water and make delicious tea. I'd remembered the area from a picnic we'd taken. I'd picked wild herbs with his mother while his father butchered a chicken and rinsed it in a cold stream for the barbecue. But as Vahid put a blanket and candles into his backpack, and prepared to drop his parents at the doctor's in town, they had had a last-minute change of heart. His father's back was no longer bothering him. His mother would massage a paste of turmeric and lemon into his aching muscles instead. There was really no need for a doctor, they'd insisted, and we'd gotten out of the car and gone back upstairs.

We move slowly through the bazaar, going over our plan again. It is nearly dark. People are rushing home from evening prayers. The chicken seller is switching off the naked light bulbs and tossing bloodied, rolled-up newspapers into the trash. Women pour water from cola bottles onto the pavements in front of their doors to cool them and make it smell like rain.

'The steps to my room are just past the kitchen,' I repeat. 'If you go the back way, you can reach it without being seen. You have to walk through a little dining room but it's always empty.'

A group of children rush past us, rolling a large tyre down the alleyway. They feed its rubber notches through their hands, hollering encouragement at each other to go faster. One of the boys slips and the children lose their footing, sending the tyre slamming into one of the shopfronts. The children collapse into peals of laughter as it bounces off and spins onto its side, their mischievous excitement joyful and infectious. Normally Vahid would pinch their cheeks, or roll up his sleeves and help them set their tyre upright. But this evening his face is fixed with concentration and he passes them, staring straight ahead.

It had occupied my thoughts last night when I lay in bed, deliberating as I tried to fall asleep. Would he take his time with me? Should I treat him with extra care? Would he like the first full sight of my (dirty, filthy) naked body or was I setting myself up to be further humiliated?

I focus on keeping my pace easy and unhurried. Vahid waits by the doorway while I check the reception desk. I imagine the staff would take pride in discovering us, eager for the reward for phoning the police. I turn back and wave for Vahid to follow. I hear his slow, careful footsteps, the light rasp of his breath. We quickly squeeze each other's hands. From this point there is no going back.

As we part, moving in separate directions, I wonder if, like me, he realises that this is where we'd first met, the place where we'd first thought so little of each other. Only feet away it had all started so innocently, with a hello and a glass of tea, a handful of sugar.

I pass through the courtyard and the waiters spot me. They are used to my returning late in the evening. They like to tease me, telling me I'll have to choose one of them to marry. That it isn't safe for a pretty girl to be out alone. Often I linger, describing the recipes I've cooked, enjoying the fierce debate that ensues. They argue and critique, thumping and shoving each other, citing the techniques of their mothers, insisting on the correct way to cook a stuffed hen or a sweet milk pudding.

But tonight I am pleased to see the courtyard is busy; a tour group are having dinner and there is a loud din of laughter, music and the clanging of cutlery. The waiters are rushing back and forth with plates and glasses, with time only to smile and wave quickly in my direction.

With my hands outstretched, I grope along the walls, feeling the cold stone beneath my palms. I reach out, taking swipes with my fingers, hoping to feel his torso, his familiar thick hair. Stumbling blindly forward, I strike upon something hard, then arms come around my waist and pull me close. '*Joonam azizam,*' he whispers and I recognise the term of affection his mother often uses with him. We hold still, his warm, damp cheek against mine, listening for the sounds of something, we aren't sure what. For the sounds of men hurrying, shouting, 'They went this way!', pointing at a boy and a girl who went up a darkened staircase together.

I grope for the cold, metal padlock that holds my doors shut and Vahid uses his cellphone to shine light on it for me. The creaking of the doors is the last thing I hear before we cross the threshold and lock the bolts again from the inside. At first we stand shyly, blinking in the darkness, uncertain what to do with ourselves. The emptiness and total privacy before us feels shocking, the two small, warm beds and neat row of rubber flip-flops on the floor.

Everything has changed now that he is in my quarters. It is I who offers him a place to sit. I pour us both water from a plastic jug. Upturned for the first time since I arrived, the second cup has a thin layer of dust on its surface. He looks around at my things, picking up books, the plastic arm-bands and exercise DVDs I haven't touched. Each item he carefully folds and replaces as though nervous to leave any evidence of his presence. It is in this same, cautious way he moves towards me. He places a hand on each of my shoulders, pressing his forehead to the back of my hair.

'*Joonam azizam*,' he whispers again, his voice coming out like a sigh. He rests his cheek against the slope of my neck. I reach behind me and wrap my hands around his waist. We stand, sticking to each other like children. The timidity, the guarded approaches, the raw feelings and gnawing away at each other, all have gone. Gently he spins me around and we stand opposite each other, feeling brave, confident in what we have to give.

He pulls a toothbrush from his pocket, asking if we might first brush our teeth. We slide our feet into the sandals and stand side by side at the basin, our mouths full of foam. The normality of it is soothing. For a minute it is as if we are back at his home. I half expect to hear his mother calling me to begin splitting open a cauliflower or his father shuffling newspapers and clearing his throat.

With the lights out it should be darker. Ordinarily I

would need a lamp to be able to read. But tonight extra lighting floods in from the hotel courtyard, overcoming even the thick curtains and sheets of paper taped over the windows. In spite of the voices outside I feel fully alone with him, forgetting about the difficulties of his being here. It makes it easier to face him, to look at his eyes and the shape of his mouth. I realise I still know so little about him, or what we are together. I know only that here men should be with men and women with women. And I know the words he whispers next.

It is strange for me to think of them as the truth. Though I know in some physical way he needs and desires me, it is different from love. I can't guess at what worth we have to each other. I know only that there is something; something scratching there. We both need someone to look at us, someone to reach out and make a claim. Just for this moment, before the world outside steps in and cuts everything short, we want to linger in the belief we are free to meet a thousand times more and do this again.

I give him my mouth and he pulls me down onto the mattress. I tell him things to encourage him. I whisper his name and hear my own, spoken warm and urgent in my ear. His skin, hidden away since he was an infant, is available to me, reacting to my touch. He smells of himself, but even more so, the scent of cologne, his warm temperature and long fingers, things I've been aware of for days. Every bit of him is familiar to me but at the same time different and new.

'Thank you for letting me into your privacy,' he whispers before pressing a condom into my hand. He needs me to guide him and tell him what to do. But aside from that small gesture that keeps us separate, ensuring we can leave no permanent imprint on each other, everything else he does is his own, the will of his hands, his own body.

I am afraid to look at the time, to acknowledge the quiet that has grown outside, the things that hasten to divide us. There is no question of his leaving, or his parents would grow suspicious. He still has to make it back outside unseen. It would be so easy, in another place, to just fall asleep together now. Instead the darkness reminds me he is merely on loan to me, that the only thing left for him to do is to return home. I watch him as he stands and dresses. He shows no embarrassment at being naked in the soft light, pulling on his jeans and his shirt.

I wrap the blanket we have been lying on around me, walking quietly with him to the door.

He strokes my cheek, turning me gently to look at him.

I can see by his face he feels it is wrong to leave me, wrong to say goodnight and part this way. I experience the same, helpless distress as always. But we are at the last station, there is nowhere further for us to go. I want to tell him, 'Don't go. Stay with me,' but these are words I cannot say. 'Please be careful,' is the most I can offer.

He turns towards the staircase, disappearing into the darkness to make his retreat home. I listen intently for the sound of his footsteps on the stone floors and hear the heavy thud of the front door close behind him.

I sit and smooth out the surface of the bed. The sheets and pillow are covered in his small, dark hairs. At first their significance is lost on me and I begin to brush them away with my hand. But we are now more to each other than either of us had imagined, in a place where we cannot thrive. I look at his hairs still clinging to my pillow and wonder whether I should gather some of them to keep. But I don't need any of that to make me remember. I will never forget any of it.

I have reached an end here. Everything has been packed. My bag has become awkward with the weight and shape of three additional tin boxes of rosewater sweets that have been stuffed and forcibly zipped inside. Vahid places my belongings in the trunk of his father's car and opens the rear door for me. We drive one last time, separated, with me sat alone in the back behind him.

We pass streets I have seen many times before, or streets exactly like them anyway. The chalky roads that haven't seen a drop of rain in months. Everything built in shades of tan and beige. The signs are still a confounding series of hieroglyphs except for the numbers, which Vahid has taught me to distinguish. The symbol for six looks like a tensed, coiled snake while the forked symbol for four resembles a medieval weapon.

If Vahid is conscious of what's coming he gives little

away. It is his nature to maintain a stoic face. I don't expect a show of emotion from him. Public indifference has always been his way.

I take a photograph of Vahid in the final moments before I leave Yazd. He is sitting next to me on a bench outside the bus station, holding in his hand the ticket he's helped me purchase.

His brown eyes are pensive and his long fingernails are curled under his cheek. I tell him if I were staying longer I would do as I've seen his mother do for his father, and cut his nails for him. What he says is, 'Don't go. Stay here with me.'

He warns me not to trust people so easily in Shiraz. That not everyone will be like him. Then he tells me he has relatives in Esfahan. That maybe, if I want, he could come and meet me there.

He presses some waxed paper into my hand. 'I bought you some halva for your trip. It is made with sesame paste and sugar, it will give you energy.'

He walks me to my bus and gives my bag to the driver to put in the hold underneath. Then he comes on the bus and helps me find my seat.

He looks at me and I don't know what to say to him. There are a few girls already seated, who stare at us and whisper.

He asks the girl sitting next to me whether she speaks English and if she can keep me company during the trip.

'Jenny, I won't shake hands with you,' he says. 'It's not

allowed and I don't want to cause problems for you.' He stands a moment longer, stares at me and tries to smile. 'Goodbye, Jenny,' he says, turns and slowly passes through the aisle and down the stairs.

'Was that her boyfriend?' one of the whispering girls asks the girl alongside me. 'Why is he leaving her all alone?'

The girl beside me offers me a biscuit. I unwrap the halva on the small folding table for her to share. I rest my head on the thick curtains that run the length of the window and the bus's engines grumble to a start.

Through the blackened windows I can't see anything. There is no possibility to see his face or wave goodbye. Everything wanted or unsaid will remain so. All that matters now is to be gone, away.

Chapter Nine

I t is an adjustment to be in the kitchen with a stranger, a man, after growing used to the meticulous calm of housewives. When I knock on Ali's door at the time he'd mimed to me with his fingers, he answers wearing only a pair of pale green underpants. He picks soil from his fingernails with a kitchen knife while I lean over the sink to scrub my hands. When I try to determine what he wants to be paid for teaching me to cook, he just shrugs his shoulders and looks up at the high, black-domed ceiling.

At the market I trail several paces behind him. I sense he is mildly embarrassed by me. Once or twice I take a photo of tiny, curled cardoons or furry quince so tender it can be eaten raw, and when I review the photos later I see him watching me, unsmiling in the background, the handles of the plastic bags full of our shopping coiled tightly around his hands. Standing in the kitchen in our matching blue rubber sandals, leaning awkwardly against the turquoise tiles, we try to plan our menus, which brings about instant disagreement. He favours guts and organs we can throw on charcoal and eat with raw onions; I prefer slow, complex wedding recipes. Heart kebabs versus rice with chicken and candied orange peel. Tongue in yoghurt sauce or a whole fish stuffed with pomegranate and herbs. Each morning in Esfahan begins in the same way. My tug on Ali's brass door knocker, a fumbled answer in faded boxer shorts followed by disgruntled negotiation and painful debate.

I don't dare remind him that I am paying. That I can thread chicken wings onto skewers any time I like. Instead I try out a technique I've learned from watching Vahid's mother, shrugging my shoulders, gently shaking my head. The effect is as if one has been supremely hurt and insulted, bullied into a choice one has no wish to make. I'm stunned to find how effective it is.

So with one hand dialling his mobile phone and the other snapping a CD of screechy music into the oil-splattered stereo, Ali orders me into the courtyard to untie bundles of herbs from the market. Sitting on an uncomfortable wooden chair, I pick the leaves from the stems one by one. It is a task that takes me nearly two hours while his hairy arms pound dainty flecks of saffron with cubes of sugar and saw hunks of meat into quarters.

All of this has been arranged by Azadeh who owns the guest house in Esfahan. She'd thrown the door open to me, scarfless, when I arrived, with the greeting, 'I've found you a cook!' But by then I'd not wanted any more invitations of this nature and felt disappointed to remember the desperate email I'd sent to her weeks before from London. It was silly, I knew, to feel nostalgic, to refuse to set foot in another kitchen, to restrict myself from learning anything more now I was away from Yazd. So I smiled and tried my best to appear grateful.

Azadeh is not like any other Iranians I've met. I like her lazy way of chatting with me while sitting in the courtyard smoking cigarettes. She pleads with me to make pesto with the basil growing rampant in her garden, declaring she'll simply die if she has to eat another 'damned plate of rice'. She has an Armenian boyfriend who brings cognac when he comes to spend the night, whose uncle comes daily to teach her to speak Armenian. She wants to spend the summers in Yerevan, where there are jazz festivals and an abundance of red wine. She shows none of the need for formalities and boundaries I've learned to expect, feels no reluctance in imposing or making demands. She enters my room without knocking to invite me out to coffee, to places with dark wood and handwritten menus where art hangs on the walls. She examines my shampoo, my soap and face cream, raising them to her nose or squirting dabs into her palm to try. One morning she drops a magazine in my lap, a copy of Italian *Vogue* another guest has left behind, thrusting a pair of scissors into my hands. She points to a photograph of a model with short bobbed hair and asks me to cut hers in the same style. I suppose I could find it rude or intrusive to be treated with such familiarity by someone I barely know. Instead I am flattered to be drawn into these everyday intimacies and requests. I chop at her long, black hair, nervously watching it fall into dark, cloud-like piles on the floor.

At first it is for her that I submit myself to Ali's lessons, to following him and feeling ordered around like a child. But I grow to like his rough, male ways and his love of meat and sinew, and he seems happy that I keep up with the relentless pounding and chopping he demands. Carrots we cut into long, fat diagonals. Slow-fried aubergines are mashed to a pulp with the flat side of a teacup. The fenugreek, chives, parsley and mint I spend hours sorting and mincing are thrown in to a pan of spluttering hot oil and toasted until they are glossy and reduced by two thirds.

I learn through Azadeh that he cooks professionally for wealthy families in Tehran, where he has a wife and three children. He is here only because Azadeh's mother is a close friend of his family and he felt obliged to come when he heard Azadeh was here alone. He'll go back to them at the end of the summer but for now he's agreed to live here and help out.

In a strange way Ali and I are almost alike. He sets up his round wooden chopping board at an angle to the two plastic colanders he uses repeatedly, one designated for the pot, the other full of peelings and scraps. I can see by how he moves that he is used to being alone in a kitchen. His entrances and exits force me to duck out of his path and when he reaches for utensils he frequently knocks me in the face. While he works his sharp elbows extend out from his sides, allowing little room for me to stand beside him. I understand that I am in second place, limited to the territory of a small section of free counterspace at the opposite end of the kitchen.

But Ali can be warm, even charming. He comes to be proud, and to like the taste, of our food, carrying it on a tray with great ceremony, in amber bowls and earthenware plates. We eat our meals in the same shady alcove each day, watched by a squadron of cats. He enjoys that I have an appetite, sometimes laughs with his mouth full as between us we eat portions for four, even six. He teaches me to tap the long slender bones with my spoon, to release the jelly-like marrow trapped inside. We smear it across torn pieces of flatbread or eat it with last mouthfuls of rice.

It is at Azadeh's urging that I try to extend my visa. She offers me extended use of my room at no charge, insisting I stay on as a guest. From now on I am to use the key she hands me on a ribbon in place of ringing the bell when I come and go. But in all honesty I tend to go out rarely, preferring the sanctuary her home gives me and the pattern that now consumes my days. The mornings see me with Ali, chopping and grinding, busy in the haze of oil that rises in the kitchen. Afternoons, by unspoken agreement, I go to her.

Sometimes we sit for hours on the roof sipping fresh lime sodas, clad in only our T-shirts, our hair flapping in the sun. We download flamenco music and jazz over her high-speed internet and light candles when the sky darkens, wrapping ourselves in wool blankets and dipping our toes into the fountain that runs the length of her courtyard. If Ali finds it all extravagant or improper, he gives little away. Or perhaps he has grown used to Azadeh and the way she conducts herself with the guests she singles out. Besides, he is outnumbered; we are two against one, which I suspect is part of the reason she wants to keep me on.

When Azadeh looks at me she doesn't see someone with a determined agenda or a sightseeing checklist, someone with a clear allocation of time. What she sees instead is a companion, someone equally uncompelled, with the same sense of ease and freedom to fill her day.

She gives me an address and a man to ask for – a government channel who owes her a favour. At the mention of her name she believes he'll stamp a new exit date in my passport, allowing me to stay beyond the original date I'd planned.

Street names in Iran follow a pattern. They commemorate milestone dates from the Islamic revolution or celebrate valiant themes of war. Every city has a street named for freedom, another for martyrdom; the largest and most important square is given over to Imam Khomeini. Occasionally streets retain the names of writers and poets, the wide, tree-lined thoroughfares named after Hafez or Sa'adi.

Vali Asr is the name of the street where the Police Office for Foreign Aliens is located, named after the prophet of time. It is here in this grey four-storey building that foreigners' visas are agreed or extended, where permits are granted or deportation orders signed.

The security officer at the entrance barks at me to fix my scarf before entering. My mobile phone is taken away and locked in a drawer. Inside there are at least four separate lines of people waiting at counters manned by officials in uniforms, not unlike old-fashioned tellers at a bank.

Though Azadeh made no mention of money, I've come prepared. I'm aware of the covert power it has. Even in the taxi here my driver had refused to pass me the change for my twenty-thousand-tooman banknote until he first had my cash firmly in his hand. By his clamped fist you would have thought he was holding back a day's salary or at least the equivalent money for a packet of cigarettes. But it meant that attention was paid to the passing back and forth of money: a lesson in what was OK and what was not.

There is little natural light in the room except what creeps in through the yellowed, dusty blinds. The room is warm and humid with the bodies of so many people. The amount of documentation they carry – from a photo card to entire folders of sheafs of paper – indicates there is a vague logic to who is standing in which line, a suggestion of some kind of order and purpose. I join the smallest queue, hoping for a quick turnaround; the man behind the counter seems flustered but efficient.

Nearly everyone here is Afghani. I recognise their accents. Their dialect, Dari, is formal and centuries old. Their Persian is that of ancient literary texts, a language once spoken in royal courts. They speak with the open, rounded vowels Iranians have long abandoned. Their vocabulary and syntax are complex and rich. None of the laziness of the standard Tehrani dialect has crept into their speech. They would never imagine saying *Iroon* instead of *Iran* as Iranians do, or referring to its capital as *Tehroon* or saying *e* instead of *ast*.

In spite of their elegant patter, or perhaps because of it, the officials here delight in bewildering the Afghanis with long, complicated words. They pass them documents full of Arabic terminology more suited to legal contracts than for instructing them on applying for the coveted residence permits they seek. Although the government has instigated a language-preservation programme called *Farsiro pas bedarim* where Arab words are singled out and replaced with Persian, it doesn't seem to be widely practised here.

The Afghanis accept their documents in a distracted

state. The men do all the talking while their wives appear to be speechless. Gradually, one by one, they shuffle away, under a shadow of confusion and defeat.

When I reach the front of the line the official looks startled to see me but his expression quickly changes to a distant one of boredom. Behind him are shelves and cabinets piled with paperwork and manila folders, cabinets that have to be prised open by the staff in order to be rifled through. On wheels and at a strange angle is an unplugged, glass-fronted refrigerator, the kind used in fast-food places to display meat for the grill. But inside there are no chicken wings or skewers of minced lamb, no pieces of liver threaded between chunks of raw onion. I want to make a joke about it, if there is perhaps some bureaucratic reason for its presence. Maybe it is an inventive place to file papers or a mechanism to transfer files from one place to another. But I know any attempt at humour would probably just agitate him, so I look down at my hands instead.

'What do you want?' he says, addressing me in the informal. His voice is unmistakably gruff and his insult plain. I remember Vahid once telling me that some Iranians strive to treat foreigners with added indifference, to make a show of being blasé and unimpressed.

As a result, I feel my Persian begin to slip. Any hope of clear, perfect sentences fades away. I mangle my tenses and forget the word for extension, saying something like 'visa prolongment' instead.

It doesn't matter, he doesn't keep me for long. A photocopied form in English is pushed towards me through the little grate at the bottom of the teller window. He shrugs when I repeat the name Azadeh has told me. Already he is looking over my shoulder at the growing line of people behind me and points me to another window, number nine, instead.

The woman at number nine looks harassed, as if any request will cause difficulties. She squints at my form as though an extension is both unique and unlikely. She asks for my passport and shoves the form inside. Pointing to the row of seats, none of which is empty, she tells me to sit down and wait. She doesn't smile and I don't expect her to.

Beneath a square clock on the wall a line of us are standing. Some have taken to sitting on the floor. Jackets are rolled into cushions. A bag of dry bread scraps is passed around. I stand watching the spot where my passport has been placed. I can barely make it out at the bottom of a stack of folders and forms stapled together. For the next hour it ascends only slightly towards the top.

In between there is the slow, confused passage of people: from the back to the front of one line and again to the back of another, new line. Sometimes people are sent scurrying away to search for a pen, to secure a hasty signature or to complete another form. More than once there is fierce yelling and shoving when they return and try to reclaim their place. In one case a couple with a young daughter challenge another man who tries to step in front of them, insisting that he'd been waiting there first. Few intervene to break up the resulting shouting match, which goes on for several minutes until they are all removed by Security and escorted outside.

The staff has begun to rotate. Working shifts end and new ones begin. The security guard who'd taken my phone and complained about my scarf earlier is gone. A younger, clean-shaven man takes his place. One by one the women employees close down their wickets, lowering metal shutters and going off to a small room to pray. The queues begin to dissolve into huddles, the huddles into a kind of human forest. I have to edge my way along the walls to see any movement or guess when they might call for me.

A woman sifts through the pile of folders under which my application is buried. Every hour or so she plucks a handful of files from the top and carries them away. Eventually my passport is moved into another metal basket. Then finally it is placed on a man's large wooden desk. He gives it a cursory glance and then scans the room for me, his eyes briefly meeting mine. Minutes later I am summoned back to window nine to collect it and the whole ordeal is over. Fifteen more days – a lifetime in Iranian visa terms.

Later that evening, Azadeh insists we celebrate. She brings out two glasses, a bucket of ice. She is studying the new stamp in my passport, which takes up an entire page.

I tell her the man whose name she'd given me had been nowhere to be found. Rather than being alarmed or confused, she absorbs the information casually, as if she'd expected nothing less. She tilts the passport to make out the signature of today's official. 'Mr Hemmatipour,' she reads aloud.

Chapter Ten

He doesn't know it, but Ali's acceptance makes it somehow easier, makes me feel less cut off than I have been. I still picture Vahid standing alone in the middle of the street where I left him, watching as my bus pulled away. I imagine him sleeping alone on the floor with his mother and father in the next room, unable to say anything, with them knowing nothing at all. By now I will have become just a memory for his parents, their lives having returned to normal, three plates put on the cloth at mealtimes instead of four.

Before coming to Esfahan I had tried to drain the life of these thoughts. In Shiraz where the bus had deposited me for the next stage of my journey, I'd aimed to find a fresh routine and move on. I'd bought myself a new coat in a style I'd noticed was fashionable, a thin crêpe-like material that hugged my waist and flared out like a dress. I went for walks to the poet Hafez's tomb each evening, where his poems were read aloud in thick, masculine voices that poured out of speakers hanging from trees. I sat on benches in gardens that smelled overwhelmingly of orange blossom and ate cups of tart lemon sorbet with noodles that crackled between my teeth.

Every day Vahid wrote to me. Brief emails, sometimes two or three in one day. In between short sentences of concern for my well-being and expressions of tenderness, he put the craving for foods in my mouth. He urged me to wait in the long lines outside the Mahdi ice-cream parlour, to eat their chewy ice cream made with orchid root and mastic that can stretch for several feet without breaking. He described the *torshi* shops in Bistodoh Bahman Square where vegetables, roots, even young pine cones are pickled, swimming in buckets of caraway seeds and vinegar. I bought cauliflower, caper shoots and tiny turnips scooped into clear plastic bags and topped up with a ladleful of sour brine. He made it so that when I ate I heard his voice in my head, missing his presence from every meal. I felt him beside me adding lemon juice or salt, tapping sugar or crushing sour sumac between his fingers.

Though I knew I wouldn't see him again, I took actions to make myself more pleasing. I bought a pumice stone to rub against my dry cracked heels, a balm to protect my lips from the sun. One afternoon, on a whim, I removed all my body hair in the shower, shaving while clumps of hair dropped to the floor. I stood afterwards in front of the mirror, examining myself, expecting to feel pleased, but instead I felt lonely and stranded, having prepared for an intimacy that would never take place.

It was strange to be on my own again. I was unused to the men in Shiraz who hissed and called out. It felt impossible to walk any distance without attracting their stares or the honking of cars or being followed in the street. One evening I counted thirty blocks while a white car drove slowly alongside me, pulling over and blaring its horn every few paces. I did my best to ignore it all, always staring straight ahead, flushed and irritated but unwilling to give in and shout back. My resolve finally broke one afternoon when two teenagers pursued me down a narrow alley, whispering obscenities and spitting sunflower shells at my feet. I prepared to make a loud scene if they tried to touch me, but there was no one around. As they closed in I reached for my camera and began taking their photographs, an act that finally sent them running away.

The sound of Vahid's voice was a comfort to me. I grew to look forward to his phone calls every evening in my hotel room. His impatience and hurried questions no longer felt brusque. Instead I enjoyed his high-energy demands for information. He wanted to know everything I'd seen and where I'd eaten. He laughed and sounded proud that I did all these things alone. In the background I heard his parents calling out greetings; sometimes his father also came to the phone. He told me they missed me, that I should come back, his words faint through the crackling of the line.

His phone calls came around nine each night without fail, until one evening they abruptly stopped. I had waited over an hour, telling myself I wasn't really waiting, and reminded myself it made sense for things to taper off. I had just started to fall asleep when I was startled by a loud banging on the door to my room. I threw on my scarf and opened it to see two men shuffling nervously on the carpet, looking embarrassed, holding armloads of screw-drivers and tape. They told me someone had been trying to call me all evening and had demanded they come up to check the wiring. They got down on their knees, turning screws and twisting cables, but not without first wedging the door open with a chair. Five minutes after they left, the phone rang and it was Vahid. 'How are you?' he chimed, his usual greeting instead of hello.

I knew he had annoyed the hotel staff by berating them. Probably he'd raised enough suspicion that my name had been logged. But it had been a long time since anyone had shown such persistence in getting through to me. I was touched by the extent of the measures he took.

In spite of this, even as we spoke I could feel myself changing, already getting back to a more rational place. I'd quietly begun in turn to scold and forgive myself for what had taken place in Yazd. For acting on feelings where there had been no one to witness or judge how I behaved.

But on that evening he opened a new chapter. He offered to come to me, to meet in Esfahan. 'I don't want to impose on you,' he said and I heard myself urging him, telling him, 'No, please come, just come.' With just a few sentences he'd thrown away all my misgivings and this questionable thing had returned to life. And instead of closing the door on what I had considered unthinkable, I was asking how soon he could be with me again.

After we hung up, I tried to imagine the restrictions we'd be under, all the things we wouldn't be able to openly do. It became clear a line would be drawn between what we had been together in Yazd and what we might become in the days ahead. On one side was the sheltered existence we'd enjoyed in his parents' home, clandestine but with safe places to flourish and hide. Now we'd be without shelter, exposed, forced out into the open, subjected to new attention and scrutiny, but without the security of any real foundation between us.

We choose Imam Square as our meeting place, a vast *meidan* the size of fifteen American football fields. We are due to meet somewhere near the fountains in the centre, opposite the breathtaking tiled heights of the Shah mosque. I pass through the stone pillars of the western entry gate, slipping into the open-air corridors that shield me from the sun. The long curved archways of honey-coloured stone resonate with the rattling of idling taxis and the giggles of schoolchildren. As I walk I hear the heavy footsteps of the turbaned mullahs Iranians call 'cabbageheads'. Their surly bodyguards force a path through by shoving people roughly to one side. Young men hopeful of an emigration romance watch out for German tourists, waiting to tell them they have beautiful eyes.

I've already dreamed this moment in my head. I know how I want it to be. I hope he'll notice my new coat, how its colour makes my eyes seem more green. At the edge of my scarf I've fastened my hair with a clip to the side to show off the streaks of blonde that have emerged from afternoons in Azadeh's courtyard, exposing my head and arms to the late afternoon sun.

It isn't lost on me, all the effort I am making, to go and meet a boy in a square on this clear blue morning. I feel a flutter in my stomach at the prospect, a nervousness that makes me light-headed. If I had anyone to tell, they might laugh at me, wilfully succumbing to courtship, here in this most hopeless of places.

I know Vahid's family have consented for him to follow me here only because it could never have occurred to them. When his father had loaned him fifty dollars and his mother had tucked a lunch of *lavosh*, cucumber, mint and cheese, into his travel bag, they were thinking of him as my host and protector. They had enjoyed the sweet, temporary nest I had made for myself in their suburban Yazdi home and smiled at my quirky Western socialisation, seeing me as bold and animated where their daughter and nieces were reserved and shy, but they had never imagined the unthinkable.

For a traditional Yazdi family, a relationship was a mathematical formula: the correct variables of age, beauty, morality and finances were entered and the output was a successful, peaceful marriage. It couldn't be, therefore, that their Iranian son could feel desire for someone six years his senior, someone who didn't come to him pure and untouched. I was an amusing visitor from another world and soon enough I should return to it, fading quietly into an anecdote brought up over tea or a postcard taped onto the fridge; a photograph kept in a shoebox. There was nothing in their minds to worry about, for Vahid could never love such a girl as me.

I see him through the crowds before he sees me. He is sitting on a stone bench, his chin tilted downwards. His brown eyes look tired and his clothes are wrinkled from the six-hour bus journey from Yazd. Lying at his feet is a worn army duffel bag and the canvas circle of a folded Iranian tent. He'd said he had an uncle in Esfahan, but he has come prepared to sleep in a nearby park among the travellers you see without money for a hotel, families who barbecue chickens and boil kettles on open gas flames. A sense of responsibility for him flares up in me. We are in this new city: together, alone.

'Hi, Jenny,' he says, looking in the opposite direction when I sit down beside him. 'Are you fine?'

He runs his fingers quickly along my hand to let me know that he is happy to see me. It has been six days since we'd last seen each other. We blush and exchange shy glances, gently pressing our ankles together. Vahid is more nervous than I have ever seen him. His face is even sterner than usual, his mouth pulled into a tight line. He tells me he has tried to dress like a *baazgashteh*, an Iranian emigrant coming back as a tourist. He wears a golf shirt two sizes too large, printed with a consulting firm's logo, a gift his uncle had brought him from America. A *National Geographic* tote bag hangs from his shoulder, a Nike windbreaker is looped around his waist. He asks for my guidebook so he can carry it openly, the front cover facing outwards at all times. He hopes by looking as if he, too, is a foreigner in this country, maybe we'll be left alone.

As we start walking it startles me to realise how out of place he is here. I feel a stab of guilt for encouraging him to come find me again, for tampering with his innocent and planned-out life. In Yazd he'd always seemed agile and in control, switching smoothly between the local dialect he used with *bazaaris* and taxi drivers, and an educated Tehrani accent. He'd been fully at ease, wandering freely, knowing every crooked lane. Now he must constantly ask for directions, pausing every second or third street. He speaks loudly, unconvincingly, to me in English, a ruse to make it seem to outsiders that we have come here together from the same part of the world.

I take him back to my guest house and introduce him as my cousin. I tuck his tent under my bed and bring him soap and a towel to wash his face. I am clueless how such a thing can be managed, ashamed at how Vahid will be scrutinised by Azadeh. When she arrives I can tell she has no time for him, that he is what she would call 'traditional' in a dismissive, derisory way. His formal courtesies and gestures she returns with minimal interest. I can see by her face she pities me for being saddled with such a relative for a companion, that it is only for me she tolerates his presence, allowing him to linger on the veranda outside my room.

I make up a tray for Vahid of the leftovers I'd cooked with Ali and we eat lunch together. We don't kiss or touch each other, but quietly dip our spoons into the same bowl and tear pieces of bread. It is enough to sit beside him, to share a meal.

Esfahan should be a romantic place to meet again, a city of pleasure gardens, wooden palaces painted with peacocks and nightingales, and a river criss-crossed with softly lit bridges. But in Iran, in this new city, we are growing accustomed to behaving like strangers.

Chapter Eleven

I t is our fifth resting place in less than an hour – the riverbanks of the Zayand e Rood. A few moments to linger among the dense plantings of *shemshod* and mulberry, then it will be time for us to move again. We sit facing the river and I count the width of five handspans between us, the distance we aim for each time we stop. I pull my scarf forward to hide the blonde streaks of my hair and avoid using my hands – the giveaway of a European background – when I speak, which I do while looking out at the horizon or down at my feet. We direct the things we tell each other to my black, pointed ballerina flats or the shoelaces of his brown loafers, matching them as best as we can with uninterested expressions. I don't imagine we are fooling anyone.

The river is dry, drier than it has been in a generation, reduced to an undulating plain of mud. Stray dogs chase each other where the water should be as high as our waists and birds peck for worms in the few puddles that remain. The Si o Seh bridge would normally see its reflection shimmering in a broad expanse of water, but now it looks like a great wall dividing some disputed land in two. The figures visible on its thirty-three arches could easily pass for border guards, instead of the families who are weaving in and out to cross from one riverbank to the other.

In the handful of days we have spent in Esfahan in each other's company, we've come to prefer the evenings over the daytimes, which to us seem harsh. When the sun is high we find ourselves most pressed upon to explain something to someone, obliged to give some account of ourselves. The sunsets mark the turning point where things become simpler, where we can at last feel marginally more free. In the growing darkness I can make out the determined line of Vahid's eyebrows and the stubborn accumulation of stubble on his cheeks despite shaving with a pocket razor only this morning.

'Let's keep the rest for our tomorrow,' Vahid says, and I smile and relax slightly to hear him speak this way.

He wipes crumbs from his face, handing me the sticky remains of a fig and honey cake we'd bought from an Armenian bakery in Jolfa. Little by little my ears have grown attuned to it, this curious Persian grammar of ownership. 'Ferdosi Street? Its traffic is terrible!' taxi drivers exclaim in between long drags on pungent cigarettes. 'Tehran? Its people are rude and its city is so dirty!'

disapproving mothers tell their children who long for the excitement of the capital.

He uses the same syntax to talk about this city and its river, its nocturnal rhythms of which we are now a part. He uses it when he refers to its people, the Esfahani, with whom we mingle. They gravitate to the same places, purchase the same snack of toasted chickpeas and melon seeds in twisted newspaper cones, pay the same heightened price of five thousand rials. They come out each evening as we do, to claim a piece of the riverside for themselves.

The long cobbled riverbanks are ideal for drawing the attention of admirers. Legions of unmarried girls patrol up and down from one side to the other, giggling and burying their heavily made-up faces in their sleeves. Young couples nestle in shadowy corners and hold hands. Students come to play chess or read French novels, printed from the internet and bound with twine. On the grassy embankments behind us a group of women in chadors lie on scraps of carpet, shoeless but in black-stockinged feet. They watch us disapprovingly, grumbling a sour-faced commentary while fumbling with the yards of black cloth they lower and raise across their mouths.

We know we don't have very long to stay here, in one place. We're already dreading the arrival of the village boys with patched-up shirts and scraggly, attempted beards who make up the lower ranks of the religious police. Nightly they scour the riverbanks for signs of illicit behaviour, jostling for bribes to avoid a trip to the police station. The only way to have any privacy or to elude the threat of arrest is through a routine of constant movement: coffee shops, small shaded parks and quiet teahouses. Each day becomes a circuit of stolen moments, whispered conversations and hands snaked together.

Sometimes we are lucky and can manage an hour. The man who runs the *halim* shop lets us monopolise a table at the back for as long we like, eating his thick, turmeric-stained purées from a flat, styrofoam tray. At the *beyrooni* shop we were less fortunate; its owner regarded me suspiciously over his scorched iron cooking drum and told Vahid he didn't want any trouble. Thrusting warm, oily packets of sheep's stomach fried with cinnamon and almonds into our hands, he shooed us away, forcing us to eat from our laps, perched on the steps of some ruined, forgotten building. Luckily for us in Esfahan there are many such places. We spread out newspapers and eat our meals in the candle-like glow of Vahid's Nokia. If we keep perfectly still the elderly men and women with diminishing eyesight who live in the quarters we frequent can be reliably counted on to pass us by.

The worst are the goodbyes each night, the fact we must spend it separately, sleeping apart. I fetch an overnight bag from his belongings kept under my bed – a clean T-shirt, a toothbrush, *barbari* spread with honey from Ali's kitchen – and we meet in the side alley outside Azadeh's heavy wooden doors. We kiss and say goodnight for what seems like hours before he begins the two-hour journey from shared taxi to shared taxi to reach his uncle's apartment on the outskirts of the city. I know his uncle's home is little more than a hotel to him, that they'll think nothing of him coming and going, of offering him a place on their floor. But each morning I feel guilty to see him looking tired and haggard from the distances he travels to and away from me.

Fearing for his safety, I dissuade him when he wants to erect his tent in the alleyway behind, wanting to be near by when I wake up, to avoid wasting time. Already there is the sense of days running out, the knowledge that in two weeks this will end. Without saying it to one another, we know the night times are preparing us for how things will be. It makes me remember something he'd written to me in an email, after I'd left him the first time in Yazd. 'I am spending beautiful times alone by myself, with my memories.' I realise I have begun to love him, that in our strange way I belong to him and he to me.

I'm startled at the appetite he now has for sex, asking for it openly, making demands. 'I need to be romantic now,' he says, his eyes full of longing. We fumble and grasp at each other like teenagers. My hands turn his hair into an unruly mess. Though there is a sense of desperation to how we are with each other, something of the formal ceremony remains. He asks first for permission, his initial approach still innocent. He is careful, always watchful for a cut-off, in case I grow uncomfortable or get spooked.

But I never say no or 'Not here'. In alleyways, next to rusting bicycles, under archways more fit for feral cats and nesting pigeons, I oblige him, denying him nothing, holding little back.

Sometimes in our anxiousness, on evenings when there are too many people walking past, too many hurried, clumsy separations and smoothing of hair and clothes, we resort to sheltering in the peace of Azadeh's hallway, pressing up against the wall amid some coats. Once I'd been mortified to hear the approach of Ali's footsteps, feeling shame at what he'd think if he found us there. To our relief he turned away at the last second and we listened to the creak of his door, the eventual turning off of the lights in the corridor. Vahid spent that night in my bedroom, on the mattress on the stone floor.

Away from Yazd, away from the presence of Vahid's parents, our being together invites suspicion and intrusive questions. People interrogate him as if he were their son or a family member, and I feel my face flush hot when I see them gesturing at me. 'Who is that girl? Is she your guest? What do you know about her past?' ask the swells of people who crush up against the table next to us and look at me like a piece in a museum. The fascinated attention I'd first enjoyed now seems like a big misunderstanding. I feel stupid and foolish for mistaking admiration for what it really is: a kind of morbid distaste. In the teahouse where we sip iced milk with rosewater; on the bus as we lean on the barrier that separates the men from women. People close in to understand our conversations, prod with curiosity and nosy whispers, observe as we enjoy our limited freedom. I pretend not to notice but I feel it everywhere.

They ask questions for which we have no answers, and we don't care to explain ourselves. For there is no term for what we are to one another. We can't sit together on buses or hold hands in the park. But we watch over and guard and feed each other, a kind of makeshift family, caught up in long and endless restraint. We manage tender nights of sex on the cold floor of my room, sleeping like lambs on the thin foam mattress, sharing sips from the plastic bottle of yoghurt and mint we leave to ferment and grow fizzy during the course of the day. We turn heart and liver kebabs over tiny barbecues, eating sheep tripe snipped into bowls of broth with cinnamon and lemon juice. As he slips from my room at first light in the morning, he turns my shoes around outside the door to ease my first steps into the new day, facing the direction of the warm, Esfahani sun. It is as if from birth he has been groomed to savour the attachment of finding a partner and wants, somehow, to bestow this devotion on me.

'Yesterday I had your dream,' he says to me now as we sit together by the river and I hear girls laughing, the Iranian girls he should prefer to me. It is their fourth or fifth circuit of strolling up and down the riverbanks, their faces long and bored, their greasy eye shadow beginning to smear.

'Listen how romantic they are speaking,' one of them says, observing us, causing Vahid's face to turn red and angry.

'What business is it of yours?' he shouts, yelling out an expletive that translates as 'you bullshit girl'. I begin to understand how quickly Iranians turn on each other without warning, even strangers insulting each other freely in the streets.

'Yesterday I had your dream and I dreamed that you were my wife,' Vahid says, turning to me. 'That you loved me the most and we were peaceful together.'

He is interrupted by shouts that come from upriver, followed by the sharp, hissing sounds we understand too well. Boys driving past on mopeds twirl circles in the air with their fingers in warning and we join the rush to gather up our things. Men extinguish their *qalyuns* and curse as they throw a day's salary of apple tobacco into the river. Couples separate and join up with cousins to form single-gender groups. Sticky plumes of overstyled hair are smoothed into place and shirtsleeves are rolled down past the elbow. A group of men in olive uniforms make their way along the riverbank, clearing the scene of people, of colour, of joy. We flee to a brightly lit street, falling into step, but walking several feet apart.

'I have an idea that could make everything OK for us,' he says when we come to a stop, finding ourselves again in the square where we'd first agreed to meet.

I listen to him, see his eyes flash when he becomes

serious, the stern, solid expression that even now has the power to intimidate and hold me at a distance. He begins to describe something I'd read about somewhere, a strange Islamic custom that would cast a hush over everything. We'd just need to obtain a simple piece of paper to be given instant standing and credibility, he explains, to be able to pass freely through the streets. I agree instantly, without hesitation, torn between amusement and intoxication at the suggestion. For in spite of our caring for one another, it is in something of an abstract, almost mythical way, the way girls fall for glamorous men the same age as their fathers or boys worship popular girls who are unobtainable. We still remain something of a joke, lacking any substance, when the marriages around us are designed and built to last a lifetime.

But this magical piece of paper would allow me to spend time fully, openly, with him, sleeping in the same hotel rooms, sharing the same benches, without fear. It would let me dissolve freely into our disobedience, trying out a life together without limitations. I imagine myself deferring to him on some of my opinions, pushing him playfully, resembling one of the braver couples I'd seen, holding hands in public, even placing my head on his shoulder. It would give us a taste of being something normal before all this comes crumbling down. For even though he says, 'You have to come back to me,' even though he pushes for an arrangement of not days or weeks but four years, I do not believe that, once I have left, we will ever meet again. It is easier just to love him now and do as I'm told. But like being temporarily sick with a fever or a daily craving for the same food, all of this must be fully explored and exhausted until it can be finally abandoned, before I step on a plane where there are no more headscarves, no more fear, no containment nor regret.

'You have to come back to me,' he says again and when I tell him I will, I feel my voice thicken, maybe out of sadness, even shame. There are no easy terms on which to consider this, but I fear he is too good and intact for me. I feel it when he asks a passing couple to take our photograph and he leans proudly towards me, not quite putting his arm around me but making it clear we are something to one another. I blush with embarrassment, folding my hands awkwardly across my waist, reluctant to peer up into their sceptical faces for the judgement I know is waiting there.

He twists a piece of tin around my finger to measure it, insisting on going to the bazaar alone. I know it is partly out of superstition that he doesn't want me to accompany him, and partly to avoid the questions starting up all over again. He returns, having spent the last of his money, holding a simple silver ring shaped like a V. It has a tiny row of diamonds, which I know must be plastic, but I like the way it feels when I try it on, new and foreign on my hand. I twist it, lining up the stones to the front, enjoying the simple symbolism it represents before tucking it away to keep in my pocket. For as much as it is serious, it also means almost nothing, just a ritual we are being forced into, the only thing that makes sense in a place where there is no other way forward.

As Vahid and I walk down the darkened alley where we usually say our long goodnights, I have questions, perhaps, but I don't feel frightened. We finalise the plans that we've made for tomorrow ('Bring your passport, a photograph, the ring that I bought you') and squeeze hands tightly before parting.

To anyone watching, we could be tour guide and tourist, fixing an itinerary to the Chehel Sotoon palace or a day trip to see the damask rose fields near Ramsar. The only clue of intimacy lies in our willingness to linger, the excessive eye contact, the quick, uneasy kiss goodnight. If all goes well, if we find the right people, this night might be the last that we'll be forced to spend separately.

Tomorrow we will set out the terms of a contract, agree an amount of time, even a price. Tomorrow I will have a husband and I will become a temporary bride.

Chapter Twelve

I worry that maybe I've misunderstood something. What if he only wants me for sex? What if I am walking into a trap? But not once after we've parted have I thought of running away or leaving him. I feel bound to see this through.

I'll let Vahid choose which of my three scarves he would like me to wear. I have wiped the dust from my shoes with a cloth, made an effort to style my hair. I've never felt so far from home. He looks tired when I meet him and I can see he is nervous too, clasping a thin plastic folder with his identity and military documents inside. He lifts my hand to his lips and kisses it quickly. '*I sacrifice myself for her,*' he says, speaking as if to someone else in the room.

I feel amazed he wants to do this with me, to sign his name on a piece of paper next to mine. Today he'll specify a length of time he wants to spend in my company, name an amount of money he'll pay me for sleeping in my bed. Though no actual exchange of money will take place and the time is arbitrary, we have no more than one week left together, I enjoy the thought of his specifying these details, finding such careful solicitude romantic.

If I have to swallow blood or tie ropes around my ankles or jump from a tall building I will do it. For in a strange way this is what I have always imagined for myself. The truth is I will do it not just because I love him, but because I have always wanted to be here, to arrive at this place. To have the sort of relationship that required me to throw myself into it entirely, demanding an intensity I would be asked to match.

As we set out we don't speak at all. The closest we come is the occasional brushing of our elbows. At first it is an accident but then I seek it out, bending my elbow further and further out by a few inches, seeking out the collision with his. He doesn't seem to notice anything, oblivious to whether we touch or not, and after a few minutes I find it unbearable. Part of me wants to stop and plead, 'Look at me,' while the rest wants to make myself small, and stay uncomplicated, and never care about brushing against him again.

Vahid is completely unprepared. He has no appointments, no real idea what to do. We spend the first hour of the day with a single address copied out of the telephone book, the destination of where our marriage should take place. On the way he gets lost several times, preferring to ask for directions every twenty seconds rather than consult my map. When he speaks to me his English becomes hurried and flustered, full of lazy, elementary mistakes. Though I know it is natural, we are both agitated and anxious, I grow irritated at the introduction of these small things. They feel a threat to undermine our plans, reminding us we come from worlds never meant to mix.

He says as much himself when we pause for breakfast, eating the scraps of bread and jam I've packed. 'It's impossible,' he says when telling me he'd wanted to phone his parents, to explain to his father what is about to happen. Instead he shakes his head, having lost his nerve, deciding it is best to keep it to himself for now. He will tell his parents later, when he feels more confident. Today there is enough to do.

I feel a wave of reluctance wash over me when he mentions his parents. I can't imagine what they will say. He'd repeated to me his mother's last words to him before he boarded the bus to Esfahan: 'Be careful. I am afraid you will fall in love.'

When we reach the marriage registration office it is completely dark. Dusty blinds are pulled halfway across the windows. All I can see is a large wooden desk covered with manila folders that might at any moment spill over onto the floor. A sheet of paper tacked to the door says 'Out of office', but there is no further information, no number to call. Vahid asks the men in the neighbouring office and their mouths hang open as if stuffed full of hard-boiled eggs. I suspect by the way they lean past him to steal glances at me that I am the first foreigner to come to this place.

I am conscious what we are asking for is seen as disreputable and cheap, something many Iranians would frown upon. For religious families a *sigheh* is considered fit merely for prostitutes or something asked for by boys who aren't serious about the future. Only girls looking for fun would agree to such a thing, the kind who allow boys to take them to motels by the Caspian Sea. And I have learned through listening that there are girls for 'fun' and girls for marriage. It reminds me of a cartoon I saw once, comparing young American and Iranian women during sex. The American is directing the man ('Faster, slower, more to the left') while the Iranian is saying, 'Don't tell anyone. Don't tell anyone.'

But not all Iranians see it this way; for some this arrangement is a creative way to skirt around the rules. 'You can just get a temporary marriage,' they tell their friends, seeing it as little more than a trite formality. It suits couples with no interest in tradition, preferring rock concerts and saving for trips abroad to a downpayment on an apartment and having children. Even university students use it in the bigger cities where rents are high, making it possible to share apartments with the opposite sex. One girl I'd read about was sharing with two male flatmates and had signed a separate agreement with each.

Still I expect to be treated with a great deal of suspicion, to receive the least possible help or assistance along our way. For that reason I'm startled when a man from the office follows after us, chasing us down three flights of stairs. He nods and grins in my direction, then presses a crumpled note into Vahid's hand. Before turning back, he pauses to linger, and pats Vahid on the shoulder in a paternal way. This gesture gives me confidence that even to strangers he comes across as innocent and brave. It reminds me why I am willing to go to all this trouble, of the qualities in him that first drew me and that now keep me here. Even though men tease Vahid when we are separated on buses. Even though they make fun of him when he travels alone. They laugh at his strange clothes and traveller's appearance, at his pockets spilling over with pens and scraps of paper. They call out to one another as he struggles down the aisle carrying his tent, '*Zaef ro bebin!*' They point and stare. 'See what an effort this village guy goes to? He came all the way to Esfahan with a tent as he is desperate for girls!' Though I know it makes Vahid angry to find himself singled out and mocked, to hear himself described this way, for reasons I can't explain each time it happens, I fall in love with him a little bit more.

For our choosing one another is out of a total absence of customary thinking. We are nothing like the East–West romances I've seen. The liaisons conceived in Egypt, in Tunisia, the Islamic beachside towns where divorced German and French women in bikinis bare themselves to local men. Liaisons hatched out while bargaining for kilims and battered copper trinkets soon giving way to rides on the backs of mopeds, first to darkened establishments on the fringes of town to hear Bedouin music, then to the desert with camel-hair blankets and packets of condoms.

Sometimes the boundary isn't clear enough and the women mistake the crafted, planned-out encounters for love, for something lasting and profound. Their promises to return intensify instead of tapering off within days. There is talk of emigration or buying an apartment. Maybe we could open a hotel together? Run a café for tourists? Occasionally women come back, with two or three suitcases, spilling off the bus since there had been no one to meet them at the airport. Among the parcels of rye bread and tubes of mustard they expect to subsist on, they have packed their dreams of a new and enchanted life. They imagine an exotic love nest with batiks and salt lamps, a ceiling fan whirring overhead. They bump their suitcases ahead of them through the dusty streets, trying to remember which one he'd said he lived in, calling out for Mohammad or Fouad or Fakhir. But only a plump wife in a headscarf answers the door, her face flushed from the chores of cooking and laundry. Three or four children will cling to her legs and waist, peering out from behind her long skirts. For a moment the women's eyes will meet and comprehension will set in, though they will likely not exchange a single word.

I suspect, like me, Vahid feels a sense of pride, a conviction that our situation is unique. The oddly appealing belief that we are slowly undoing ourselves by crossing a line that was never meant to be crossed.

I suspect, like me, Vahid feels that the mere suggestion of our marriage carries a freakish note of scandal. But though it is exciting and reckless and perhaps not to be taken seriously, it appeals to Iranians who crave drama. Stall keepers, ladies on shopping trips and high-ranking military officials reach into their purses and pull out their cellphones, eager for the chance to be an accomplice. They call their husbands, sisters, neighbours – everyone they know – to try to assist us. I watch them peer over Vahid's shoulder as he writes down the name or address they give him, or the phone number of the person they promise can help. Their faces glow with happiness to see their contribution to our growing pages of scribbles, crossed out one by one as they lead to dead ends.

I'm aware that half the information we're given will be false. That Iranians would rather give incorrect directions than appear inhospitable and say, 'I don't know.' Streets and alleyways we should pass fail to materialise, the right turn we can't miss never appears. Half the numbers we dial are incorrect; some don't exist at all. Sometimes people call us over and I sense they just want to get a good look at us: the Yazdi boy with old-school manners and the foreign *teflaki* he is dragging around. I have practically nothing to add to these conversations; all I can do is smile and tap my heart in gratitude, a gesture I have learned from watching Vahid when he thanks the people who have fed us, walked a few metres alongside us to show us the way, told us not to worry, given us reassuring nods. I say long Persian thank-yous of 'Don't be tired' and wish for their hands not to ache. I sip their sugary cups of tea, worrying that we are losing yet more time.

At last Vahid manages to get through to someone who sounds official. A step closer to the document needed to make us legitimate. A woman on the telephone asks if we have identity documents, if we can come for an appointment that afternoon. Vahid speaks clearly, spelling out our names, and when he gets to mine there is a long pause. He repeats the word 'Canadian' two or three times. I can see by his face she is using the same words we've heard several times today; she is explaining the reasons why 'it's impossible'.

She tells him she can do nothing for us but gives him the phone number of someone else she says can help. Vahid's face clouds over when he repeats the words 'special mullah' and begins to write the number down.

We agree with the mullah to meet at an address on the outskirts of the city, which we must take a taxi to reach. The buildings here are charmless, ugly high-rises. Water gushes through open canals running down the length of the streets. Vahid consults the address he has taken down on the phone, squinting to read his own hasty handwriting. It leads us down an alley where the balconies are strung with laundry lines, where sheets and towels flap overhead.

I follow Vahid down a dusty passage to a small square, where a scrawny dog with no tail lies curled in a pool of sunlight. The dog tenses, ready to flee, equating the approach of humans with being pelted with stones.

Vahid telephones the mullah to tell him we're here and soon after he comes out of one of the buildings. He is heavy and walks with a lumbering gait; his long beard is slightly scraggly and unkempt. His dark, sombre robes nearly reach the floor and a twisted black turban sits atop his head. The sunlight glints off a ring on his right hand, a large silver band with a square black stone. As he approaches I can't work out whether he looks paternal or sinister. I glance at Vahid for a clue, expecting him to share something of my trepidation, but he has gained special powers; there is an unmistakable confidence in the way he stands. This keeps me rooted to the spot and I inhale deeply, holding my breath, preparing myself for the anticipated glare of speculation and disdain.

From his jacket Vahid pulls out a small handful of flowers and hands them to me, white blossoms that have remained surprisingly fresh despite hours pressed up against the inside of his clothes. It is a gesture to make this moment special, to compensate for the dust, the flies, the sewer water draining past our feet. But he needn't worry; this is perfect for me, this hurried, practical manner of doing things I have known all my life – here in a place where both of us know almost no one, where not a single family member is present to watch.

I gaze at the bold look of pride on his face and everything feels so bright and sharp. I want to tell him, 'I love you,' something he's never heard me say. But I know now is not the time for such things. There is something unsentimental and formal about what we are about to do. Only a few, spare words are required of us now. All of our public intimacy has been expressed like this. Are you hungry? Do you need to sit? Can I carry that for you? These enquiries are the proof we are looking after each other, that we are not on our own, not deprived. Indirect shows of affection have come to make sense: love faintly disguised as concern. I suspect even if we were anywhere else – in Rome or Paris, where couples kiss openly in parks or on benches – we would keep up this careful, matter-of-fact way of speaking. Anything more would been seen as tactless and I have learned not to be that way.

'It shouldn't take long,' the mullah assures us, 'just a few minutes.' He asks for our names and shakes Vahid's hand. He tells Vahid we look nice together. 'A nice couple. A very nice couple indeed.' We stand in a kind of huddle with me facing him and Vahid leaning in on the other side. The mullah is so close I can see the pores on his face, his oily nose glistening in the bright light.

In a voice less stern than I expect it to be, he speaks as if on autopilot but in a kindly way. He talks to me as a consoling doctor might, one who'd already seen dozens of patients that day. He asks me to repeat phrases in Arabic, words that are incomprehensible to me. No explanation is given. Vahid translates nothing. He simply stands close and smiles in encouragement, watching the contortions of my lips.

At first I think this is our exchange of vows, but then Vahid keeps trying to cut in and speak. There is a burst of noise from the apartments up above, the sliding open of dozens of windows echoing down into the streets.

'*Haji Agha,*' Vahid interrupts finally, asking how much the ceremony will cost. It is then I understand the sentences had been about acknowledging God and Mohammad as his prophet: a quick, hurried conversion to Islam. I feel a bit startled and humiliated for not having grasped what was taking place. I make my quiet peace with the idea, knowing it can be cast off afterwards, having refused religion all my life.

'How much do you want ... for helping us?' Vahid repeats again, using the politest formal grammar. The mullah and Vahid stand aside, counting on fingers and taking turns raising hands in the air for emphasis. Again Vahid is clapped on the back, again he is jostled as a father does a child. But this time it doesn't feel good to me. Instead I realise how vulnerable and desperate we are.

I stand in the street, resigned to the weight and the oddness of it. Children are beginning to gather, to point at us and laugh. I haven't had much chance to look around me until now; my attention has been taken up with the respectful positioning of my scarf. I'd hate to be sent away on a technicality after having travelled all this way. I notice for the first time there is a butcher's shop on the corner. I can smell the raw meat, see the buckets full of chipped pieces of bone. A few carcasses dangle, circled by flies, swaying back and forth in the hot wind.

'Women are like the mulberries,' a man once told me, 'they attract all the flies and the wasps. You must find yourself a bee,' he said, leaning across the table and staring right through me, 'to chase the flies and the wasps away.'

'It shouldn't take long, just a few minutes.'

There are two goats tethered to a post outside the butcher's. They look back at me with their striped, rectangular eyes. These will be the only witnesses to my strange, thrown-together marriage, a fact they confirm by shitting warm, half-digested grass. I want to untie their ropes or at least scratch under their chins, to show them a little kindness on this bewildering day.

The voices grow louder. I hear the mullah laughing. He tells Vahid that if he is from Yazd he must be rich. He insists on five hundred dollars, the equivalent of a typical month's salary, to give us the document that will set us free. He talks at length of the risk to his reputation and after a while I stop listening.

'If she commits any crimes I'll be held responsible,' he gestures, turning to me. 'It will be my name on your certificate. I can't do it for less than three hundred dollars, that's two hundred less than I normally charge: a special price for you because you are such a nice couple and both so young.'

The fact Vahid is arguing isn't for me, or only a small part of it is. His pride dictates that he must deal with this himself, to ensure his time with me cannot be taken away.

How many other people have stood here, I wonder, shooing away the same flies in this same hot wind? Young couples sneaking down from Tehran, widows turned occasional prostitutes, lonely businessmen from the ports in the south needing a fix? How many of them have surrendered envelopes with five thousand toman in crisp notes to this man in exchange for his special discounts and his 'very nice couple indeed'?

Both of us want only one thing: for him to stop insisting and throwing wrenches into our plans. I keep hoping for his face to soften, for him to throw his arms in the air and say, 'Oh, all right, thirty dollars it is.' For though I have the money, it's not for me to do, to pay for our marriage myself. Such a thing would be worse for Vahid than our not marrying at all.

Nothing more is said, the negotiating ends. We round a corner and are back in the busy street. I can see Vahid is upset and his dignity wounded. My mouth is dry from not speaking. My eyes are becoming red from the sun and the dust.

How out of place and weary we must appear. Not at all like a couple hoping to be married. Walking rather than being ferried or driven. Hot and dusty instead of groomed and composed. I feel foolish, like a naive teenager, blinded by silly notions and gestures of love. The traffic, the sore feet, the hair I'd fixed in a special way, the dizzying, humiliating knocking and calling, only to be told again, 'It's impossible.'

For a moment I think maybe I've lost him, that he'll begin to turn away from me. I feel like crying out of exhaustion and despair, the solid ground we'd just begun to walk on beginning to shift away.

'Maybe the world isn't ready for us,' I tell him.

'But maybe it doesn't need to be this way,' he says. 'I still want to come everywhere with you and stay at your side. I will stick to you until it is time for you to leave.'

No two people look more sad or more shy. I reach over and touch his cheek. We are in the middle of the pavement, with people and cars rushing past. 'I love you,' I tell him. He smiles and gives a little nod. A tear rolls down his face. I slip on the ring that I carry in my pocket. Already one of the diamonds has come loose, threatening to detach and come away.

A car pulls up alongside us, honking its horn. A young man lowers his window and leans out. 'Do you need a lift into town?' he asks. 'Let me take you. I'm going that way.' Out of politeness Vahid climbs into the front beside him and I sit on my own in the back. The man smiles at me in the rear-view mirror, then turns and begins speaking to Vahid.

'I was in the butcher's,' he says. 'I saw you both with that clergyman. Everyone knows him in our neighbourhood.

We have a name for him: "Haji Poolaki". All he cares about is money. He is famous for demanding bribes. We see some couples paying up to eight hundred dollars, and even then he tries to make them pay more.'

He tells us it's good we didn't pay him, that one day such men will disappear from Iran for ever. We offer him some money for the ride before stepping out of the car, but he won't hear of it and smiles while shaking his head. Once more Vahid is patted on the shoulder like a younger brother. 'Good luck,' he tells us and drives away.

It is nearly three in the afternoon when we find ourselves wandering the streets again. We are both quiet but vigilant, looking around, as if some sign of what to do might show itself. We pass car repair shops where orange sparks fly onto the pavement. Metal pieces are sawed and banged together so loudly that we move away and plug up our ears. I'm accustomed to following Vahid, to his leading the way with some destination in mind, but for the first time it feels as if there is nowhere for us to go. As we walk we are both silent and angry, stubbornly having set our minds on something that hasn't worked out. We'd been swept along on our thrilling act of rebellion and have landed flat on our faces, unfulfilled.

We avoid talking about how we will manage tonight. Or tomorrow. About what to do with the bus tickets to Kashan in my hand. We'd made the reservation together just this morning to stay with a family there. The name of their house, Noghli – the sugared almonds Iranians throw at weddings – had seemed perfect. They were a close proximity to the rose fields where damask petals are harvested. It had seemed the ideal place for us to begin.

My stomach is growling. We haven't eaten since breakfast. The day has been too urgent to think about food. But as we pass a stall with a few wooden stools on the pavement, we stop and decide to buy something to eat. I'm disappointed to learn it sells only puddings, something I have no appetite for. But as I lean over to see the simmering pots of creamed rice and thickened milk, I succumb to my hunger and point to a pot of bubbling *fereni*. It is a mixture of milk, cardamom and rosewater thickened with rice starch, something Vahid's mother had taught me to make. It had been the first cooked food Vahid and his sister had consumed as babies. She'd prepared it almost daily when they were children. I remember her eyes filling with tears as she whisked it with her fork, mimicking how they'd opened their infant mouths for the incoming spoon. I'd stepped forward to take her place at the stove as she wiped her eyes with her sleeve.

We drop onto the stools, exhausted. We eat ravenously, barely stopping to look up. Quickly we reach the bottoms of our plastic cups and Vahid rises to buy each of us a second. The afternoon sun cuts down with a fierce, radiating heat. The trees overhead provide little shade. A row of 'fashen' shops are reopening for after-lunch business, and mannequins are being carried horizontally and propped up in the street. Muscle shirts with lopsized logos for the men. Pink trenchcoats and *rousaris* for the girls. A loud mix of trash disco and *bandari* goatskin drums blares from the speakers inside. It is getting close to the end of the school day. A few moms and children are trickling in among the older men who drop their cigarette butts on the pavement.

'*Salut!*' An eager voice booms out. I squint to see a man waving at me from across the way. He is dressed in the same long robes as the mullah who'd shunned us earlier, but he must be twenty years younger at least. His face is chubby and round.

Gingerly he moves through the crowd. He lacks the arrogance of the other religious men I've seen. In spite of the heavy clothes he is wearing, his step is lively and upright. He reminds me of a student on his way to a lecture.

'*Vous parlez français?*' he asks, grinning down at me. When I nod, he drops his leather satchel at his feet, taking Vahid's vacant seat next to me.

He speaks to me in an overly intimate manner. Patting my arm. Staring into my eyes as he speaks. Did I know Paris? Wasn't it the most beautiful city in the world? Had I stood in front of Notre Dame at sunset and seen the way the light reflects off those thousands of pieces of coloured glass?

It's been years since I've set foot on the continent, since I'd first admired the places he describes. I feel a hint of annoyance at being reminded of them now, bits of information and detail having nothing to do with here. They come from a world I've temporarily but fully abandoned. And now they seem intended to pull me away.

I suspect this is his usual way – that, in spite of his obvious choice of career, he would be no different if he were a barber or one of the merchants in the bazaar. Passers-by glance over at us. But he takes no notice or perhaps he doesn't care.

I am not really surprised by how he is acting. A lot of people I've met while abroad behave this way. There is a quantity of European imagery – cathedrals, canals, quaint villages with wooden houses and red geraniums blooming from every window box – that travellers tend to cling to, recalling them with tremendous nostalgia.

As superficial as his interest is in me, I nod and shake my head in turn at his questions. In any case he doesn't seem concerned with what I think. He inhales sharply, pressing fingers and thumb together, rolling his eyes skywards in a dreamy way.

A tingling begins in my stomach and spreads through my body. I search the crowd for Vahid's face. He is just heading back to me, his hands full with the sticky-sweet cups he is carrying. When he sees us he stops in his tracks. The young mullah is still grinning lazily, swooning like a teenage girl. I need no instructions. I know what to do. Quietly, carefully, I lean towards him.

'You want to get married!' he exclaims. 'But why? To whom?'

Vahid steps forward, extending his hand with a greeting of 'God be with you' and a knowing smile breaks on the young mullah's face.

'Aha!' he exclaims. 'I understand. It is a terrible state to find yourself in. I remember when I was studying in Paris it affected me too. For months I was surrounded by beautiful European girls, my body burned with sexual desire that I needed to satisfy.'

I listen, stunned, my eyes moving from him to Vahid. I realise by Vahid's blank face he hasn't understood a thing. I tilt my head to the side quickly and smile at him. Cautiously, he pulls up a third stool.

'Would you help us?' I ask the mullah, still speaking in French. 'We need some help to keep ourselves protected.' Swallowing hard, I explain we've had a lot of problems with the police in Yazd, that we would like to do things right 'by God'.

'Of course!' He smiles again, looking delighted. He reaches for his satchel but Vahid is ready, passing across his notebook and pen.

'How long would you like to be married for?' the mullah asks. 'You said you are leaving in one more week?'

I turn to Vahid, speaking to him in English, before turning back to the mullah to relay his answers in French. Somehow it suits me to be sitting between them, translating, on one side his eager smile and on the other Vahid's bewildered expression.

'Four years,' I reply, giving Vahid's answer.

The mullah looks at me as if we've lost our minds. 'Go for one year, it is enough,' he says. 'After that you can just do another one.'

I don't want to threaten our fragile footing, so I agree to the terms. 'Now how much will he pay you?' he asks, his pen flying across the page.

I look at Vahid. 'Well, it really isn't about money. He doesn't need to give me anything.'

'Bah. You must ask for at least one thousand dollars,' he insists.

'*D'accord,*' I agree, nodding. I can see Vahid squirming with curiosity, biting his lip.

He turns to Vahid and offers the pen, showing him where he should place his signature, next to the space that awaits mine. Below, the mullah has written his name and the address of the *madresseh*, the theological college, where he is studying Islam, then his phone number. If anyone should question the authenticity of our situation, we must tell them to contact him directly, he says.

While Vahid is signing a crowd has formed. Large numbers of passers-by have stopped in the street. Several more are gaping at us from their cars. I try to seem nonchalant, to keep the relief and excitement from flushing my cheeks. People appear desperate to peer over the mullah's shoulder to find out what is going on. I look away, fighting to keep the blush down.

Suddenly it is over, the document is carefully folded and tucked away, the whole ceremony ending as abruptly as it began. The mullah stoops to gather his belongings, waving eagerly as he turns to go. *'Bonnes relations sexuelles,'* he wishes us, his robes flapping as he walks away. In his wake, he leaves us, suddenly, a family, the plastic cups still in our laps. Beside me sits my new husband. Beside him, his new, temporary, bride.

Kashan is the first place where we'll truly know no one. No aunts or uncles. No cousins' floors for Vahid to sleep on. When he spoke to his mother, he told her he'd be staying in a cheap dormitory for travelling students, a lie she willingly accepts without question. I'm amazed she suspects her son of nothing, believing that he will return to his parents more or less the same as when he'd left. It gives me a strange momentary surge of power, to be tearing apart their dormant, decades-old arrangement.

We nearly don't make it. To catch the bus we have to run across a pedestrian bridge and down another flight of stairs. I was worried Vahid would knock someone over with his red tent, which threatens at one point to fall off his shoulder and tumble away. Waving fiercely and out of breath, we arrive to find the bus engine is already rumbling.

Quickly, we push our bags into the hold and the driver slams it shut with a bang. He motions for us to get on and drops his cigarette, crushing it under his shoe.

We climb onto the bus and it is full this time, unlike the nearly empty bus I'd taken from Yazd. There is a mix of elderly people and students. Some of them are already dozing off with their heads pressed against the windows, while others are lost in a world of earphones and video games.

We find two empty seats next to each other and collapse, relieved and still out of breath. Drawing our knees up into the small space is the very opposite of confinement; for once a wide-open world of possibility seems to be spread out ahead of us. Though we haven't explicitly called this a honeymoon, we feel the same change of status, the same sense of stepping out as a single, joined-up force.

We hold our tickets for the driver to inspect, and he makes several trips up and down the aisles. I can see by his hesitation he plans to separate us, and is looking for how to rearrange things. He believes he is protecting my reputation, by insisting Vahid move to a seat at the back. Normally Vahid would move automatically, without question, migrating towards the back of the bus. But the existence of a piece of paper has made us bold, more confident, so Vahid remains at my side, defending his place. The driver paces the length of the aisle and Vahid reaches for his backpack, preparing to leave.

The driver returns, pausing, studying us for a moment. Perhaps he can already detect something familiar, something close. He mutters something to Vahid and gestures, informing him he can stay where he is.

The sun is setting, the sky a deep pink. The two-hour journey will pass largely in the dark. The bus pulling away feels like an achievement in itself, after such a difficult day. Vahid leans across and I hear him singing, something he usually does only at night, when we are alone.

His singing fills me with the same combination of belonging and detachment it's always provoked, the same nostalgia whose origin I can't trace. The things that defined my life in London take on a quality here that makes them seem brittle. As if, were I never to go back to them, there would be no imprint or trace that I was there at all.

Chapter Thirteen

Vahid is teaching me to talk dirty. He urges me to be aggressive, even to shout. My polite enquiries, he insists, must now be spoken in the command form, a tense I've never had cause to use.

When I try to respond, he glares at me, scribbling notes with a notebook and pen. He waves me away dismissively, tutting and lifting his nose in the air.

I scarcely recognise him when he acts like this, speaking sternly and raising his voice. No matter what I say, he is cold and unsympathetic, voicing angry, confused and never-ending sentences full of cryptic, literary words.

For hours he tests and provokes me in Persian. He measures my persistence, my vocabulary to demand and insult. I subject myself to his constant rejection and apathy, searching my brain for the words to fight back.

'*Chera!* Nonsense!' I protest when he declares there is nothing he can do for me. 'I know you can, you are just being lazy,' I retort. I would normally never dream of addressing anyone in this manner, but in Iran I am learning it is often the way.

The reason for this is a consequence of failure. An attempted second visa extension in Rasht. We'd been told it was the easiest place in the country, a guaranteed certainty, a matter of ten dollars and an hour's time. The official there was a retired naval officer who cherished the opportunity to help the rare foreigner who washed up on his doorstep. We sat for eight hours squashed in the back of a taxi to get there, on roads that clung perilously as they curved around the edges of mountains. Twice I'd had to ask the driver to stop so I could climb out and be sick at the side of the road.

I couldn't explain where it had all gone wrong. It had started on a perfectly pleasant note. The man, Mr Ehmadi, had smiled when we'd first arrived, ushering us into his office. The plush leather chairs seemed to exhale as we sat on them, our knees brushing against a polished rosewood coffee table. The walls were covered in maps and posters of the surrounding region – endless rolling green hills and tea plantations. This is where Iranians come to craving humidity and rain, an area they simply called *shomal*, meaning 'north'.

When I mentioned the possibility of an extension he waved his hand broadly. He picked up my passport and asked whether I'd like an extra month, or even six. It was no problem, he said, either way, there was nothing to worry about, it could all be done. Then he moved towards a kettle and a set of porcelain cups, and said we'd proceed on that matter in just a moment. First, he insisted, I must taste the tea from the new season, grown in the hills just beyond Rasht.

But in the end, neither of these things happened. Instead he stopped suddenly, his hand in mid-air. He set down his kettle without filling it and turned his attention to Vahid, his manner stiffening as if he had remembered something unpleasant. In his first, formal recognition of Vahid, he seemed to be already condemning him. 'How do you know this woman?' he demanded, a cold scrutiny entering his voice.

I interjected with talk of an itinerary, a pretend reason for needing a few more weeks. I mentioned the Caspian Sea and the names of villages I'd read about in the Alamut valley, with traditional houses made of stone, capped with straw-thatched roofs.

It felt pathetic trying to deceive him. But in any case he had little interest in what I had to say. His eyes were focused on Vahid, studying him, judging him, weighing up an outcome in his mind.

At first Vahid pretended to be my translator, a casual companion, concerned with helping and acting on my behalf. What more could he say? That I was his girlfriend? His wife? Such a possibility was so remote, it was impossible to express.

They began speaking so quickly that I couldn't follow.

Vahid looked calm, if somewhat overwhelmed. But their voices were soft and measured, so I was sure there was nothing to fear.

Then Mr Ehmadi said something remarkable. 'Do you want to marry an Iranian?' He turned, addressing me. I looked at Vahid and back at him. I presumed I'd missed something in their exchange, that somehow Vahid had let our intimacy slip. 'Which Iranian do you want to marry?' he said to me without waiting for an answer. I felt heat rising to my cheeks. And then stupidly, out of confusion, thinking it was what I should do, I gestured at Vahid.

'We can do nothing for you here,' he said flatly, passing me back my passport, his 'It's no problem' disappearing like smoke in the air. 'You'll need to go back to the people who gave you your first extension. I cannot help you here. I'm sorry.'

The prospect of revisiting the place I went to before is daunting. And now there is no question that I must go alone. I dread the idea of staring again into the glum faces of the officials in Esfahan and pleading for two more weeks. It is no longer just a matter of asking and waiting, nor simply filling in another form. With two stamps already in my passport, a request for a third is certain to arouse suspicion, which is why I must now learn to stand my ground.

I know I am getting close when Vahid breaks out of character, his grimace changing into a proud smile. He nods enthusiastically when I tell him I'm going nowhere without my extension, that my plane ticket is fixed and cannot be changed. I have even inherited some of his gestures, picking up some of his traits. The rapid shaking of my head when making a point, the sharp angle at which I now fold my arms across my chest. I catch myself drumming my fingers on my elbows, a characteristic habit I've seen his mother and father make, and which I too now use to indicate haste.

Nevertheless this visit provokes a certain anxiety. I know there is truth in what I've heard: though there was once a time of strict rules and etiquette in Iran, this is fast becoming a thing of the past. The former politeness that ruled daily interactions is now viewed as weakness. Formality and elegant language have been scrapped. Being brusque and abrupt equals power in the new, rising Iran.

On the day, I dress as if going to war. My scarf clings tightly around my head and neck. I wear my darkest clothes and tug the sleeves of my cotton shirt down to my wrists. I pull black socks over my feet before putting on my thin, flat shoes, the kind of awful combination only my grandmother would think to do. My bag is filled with enough water and sunflower seeds to last out the whole day. I walk alone to the top of the street where the shared taxis swerve in and out in search of passengers, and shout, '*Vali Asr,*' in the hope of getting one of them to stop.

The driver who picks me up doesn't stop for anyone else. He drives me all the way alone. Out of kindness, I suspect, he lets me take up the full width of the back seat without the additional six passengers who would customarily fill every possible space, scooped up from street corners en route.

When he sees where I am going, he looks sympathetic, mumbling, 'Be successful, God be with you,' when he returns my change.

The building is how I remember it from before. The same white, square ceramic tiles. The same wood-veneer panels lining the walls. I greet the security guard at the entrance, whom I recognise, by saying good morning in Persian, and he looks at me as if I had done something astonishing and impressive.

Though I recall the procedure from last time, I hesitate when he insists I hand over my cellphone. It is my one lifeline to Vahid in case I run into trouble. Now I am truly cut off and on my own.

I remember coming here just two weeks before, a lifetime ago, when the surroundings had been so unfamiliar. At that stage my independence was unquestioned; Vahid had been left behind. The fact that I was moving on alone, in a new city without him, visiting a government office unaided or assisted by him, had only confirmed that fact.

But at the thought of it my throat tightens. I had not known certain things about myself. I hadn't known how much I liked, even longed, to be part of a family, enjoying the noise and the constant demands. I'd come to relish living in a house full of artefacts and possessions, melding into a life that wasn't just about me. Vahid's pursuit of me touched me, and I took pleasure in the feeling of being claimed. These things proved – with more force than the ring on my finger, with more force than our secrecy and hiding – how much had changed since then.

Yet as gratifying and exciting as it often seems, I know the whole situation is flawed from the start. Perhaps this mess with my visa is a sign to get out. In truth Vahid will never belong to me fully. He'll always be foremost some-one's brother, nephew, uncle or son. I'm not sure I could ever adapt to such a way of living, to sharing him in such a fractious way.

It crosses my mind that now may be the perfect excuse to disentangle myself, that maybe it's better not to fight. It would be an easy thing to hide in, the odds were unfor-giving. And yet, perhaps because of this, the idea of giving up upsets me even more.

In the main room I find the same scent of dust and lack of light. The unexpected silence of one hundred people jammed into a small space. Though I have come early, today is busier than last time, the lines already disinte-grating into a jumble of waiting people.

I march up to one of the teller windows and rap on the glass, startling a woman behind who is sorting through a mountain of papers. She looks annoyed but I lean in closer, placing my hands in the gap under the window to ensure she cannot slam it shut. I thrust my passport through the grate and say, 'Two weeks' extension,' then, because I cannot help it, I also say, 'Please.' I'm aware of the audacity of my behaviour but it seems to be working because she takes my passport and writes down a few details without looking at me. Then she calls a man over, muttering a few words in his ear.

He begins flipping through my passport, fingering every page, examining every visa. He arrives at the one that was stamped by this office only a few weeks ago, and lingers, studying it.

I remember what Vahid had told me about the officials working here, that I should take note of their rank. The person I was looking for would have at least three stars sewn onto his shoulders. This man has only two.

'No extension!' he growls at me. But he doesn't know who he is dealing with. I begin my memorised script of demands and refusals to leave, knowing how absurd I must sound. The Afghani women gaze at me wide-eyed in astonishment and flash their gold teeth. The men stare at each other and scratch their heads. But shame is something I left at the door and I tell myself they must at least partly be cheering me on.

It turns out the young soldier with two stars is easily exhausted. He hands me my passport and directs me to another line. I feel nervous and excited at my progress. I might be out of here by lunchtime. I'm already imagining what Vahid and I might eat to celebrate. There is a man with a stall near the park who roasts beets in their skins, directly on coals. If you ask nicely he will peel them, cut them into quarters and squeeze a half a lemon on top. In my mind I am digging a wooden spoon into my second when I realise I've been taken for a fool. After twenty minutes the teller's window where I'm standing is still vacant and dark. The soldier has sent me to the line to nowhere.

I suspect this is a tactic they use to wear down troublemakers, or at least to separate the wheat from the chaff. I've never thought of myself as a nuisance before. Now is the time to start.

I reach for the paper I have folded into a square in my pocket. It's scribbled with vocabulary I might need today. I consult it a few times, though I know it by heart, and formulate my next plan of attack.

A dirty light is filtering through the windows. More people are wandering in, sitting and standing in disorganised circles. Everyone seems doomed to wait. To the left is a room that looks unused, its doorway hung with a shabby curtain of black velvet. I step closer and peer in, carefully sliding the curtain to the side. The room is empty except for an abandoned desk. My heart sinks. I am lost for ideas. And then I see it: the battered meat refrigerator. The same one I'd noticed two weeks before.

It had likely broken down a few weeks or months earlier and been shoved here out of the way. A layer of fine dust suggests it has already been waiting some time for repairs or its inevitable disposal.

A diversion. That's what's needed. I hear chairs scraping

and then deep, male voices from above. I turn the meat cabinet gently. It creaks and the glass panels wobble. I pull it as far back as possible for a good trajectory, then slide it back and forth a few times to test the wheels. If I'm lucky it will clear at least half the room. With a deep breath I push it as hard as I can and then slip through the curtain to watch from the side.

The meat fridge sails past window tellers nine, eight, seven and six, its glass rattling violently while its plug drags along the floor behind. With a bang, it crashes in between windows four and five before rebounding with equally impressive speed.

It is almost beautiful to watch, the bodies dashing out of the way, darting aside to clear a path. The divisions between people become just a single loud mess of black cloth and plastic sacks.

Men in tan, starred uniforms appear from everywhere, attempting to bring the fridge under control. The crowd are quick to laugh as they begin to tie it with ropes, like an animal needing to be restrained. The yelling and chaos make me tipsy with exhilaration. I've succeeded in creating an ordeal, but not so much as to make me forget my purpose. One by one, I scan the shoulders of the soldiers, looking for a man who will be able finally to help me.

I begin to worry seriously that what I want is impossible, that I have no chance of success. And then I see him in the corner, looking tired and somewhat annoyed by this recent disruption. I take a deep breath and walk over to his desk.

It takes a few moments before he looks up from his papers. He doesn't recognise me and at first he can't see all the fuss. Then he flips through my passport to the place where he signed his name: Mr Hemmatipour.

He shakes his head and begins to open his mouth. He wants to tell me he can do nothing for me. But this time I am ready for him.

'Of course you can give me more time! I know you can!' I protest.

'What do you expect me to do?'

I make reference to his power, a man in his position. 'Think of your reputation!' I exclaim.

I imagine it is some of the rudest, broken Persian he has ever heard coming from a foreigner. Hemmatipour looks as if he isn't sure whether to get angry or laugh. I see what I hope is the twitch of a smile in the corner of his mouth.

He takes his calendar and begins counting. Then he examines his own signature once more. Just when I think I have broken him and will finally be victorious, he shakes his head and hands me my passport.

I've learned a new trick, which I'm forced to employ. I refuse to take back my passport. It dangles from his hand between us. I take a step backwards, shake my head and again begin my imploring accusations.

By this stage I have a minor audience, both of Afghanis and of the other officials. I accompany my statements with sweeping arm gestures, for dramatic effect. I don't know much about how these things are done so I try to tread the careful line between victim and righteous. The crowd appear to back me up. I hear generous tuts and murmurs of sympathy.

Hemmatipour seems baffled by me. I can tell he has no clue what to do. With a mob on my side he can no longer shove me away or call someone to have me forcibly removed. An awkward minute passes while he rubs his chin thoughtfully. Then he reaches for his phone and turns away. I hear the words for 'difficult' and 'making problems'. After he hangs up he points upstairs and tells me that an official on the floor above will speak with me.

Go upstairs. Is it code for 'You are causing trouble'? What is the significance of this stage? Hemmatipour presses my passport into my hand and the expression on his face reads, 'Let's see how our head honcho deals with you.'

I am led upstairs where I don't meet a soul. Everything feels out of bounds. The desks are empty, the offices enormous. No sign of the endless bureaucratic mess that rules downstairs. Whatever happens here is swift in nature – a fact that makes me worry I've gone too far.

I take a seat in the hallway and listen for a clue of what will come next. It is so quiet I could hear a pin drop. Most of the doors are closed. I wonder whether these are the kinds of places people go to, never to be heard from again.

Eventually a door opens and a man steps out. His feet

make a scuffling noise on the polished marble floor. He looks startled to see me and then, maybe embarrassed at being caught off guard, he waves his hand hurriedly for me to follow him.

He leads me to an office where two men are sitting, one of them behind a large, tidy desk. Both are much younger than I expect them to be. They can't be more than thirty-five at most. The man behind the desk motions for me to sit, extending his hand and gesturing to the seat opposite. I find their male chivalry consoling. They don't smile but they don't scowl at me either; instead they pass their eyes over me, taking in my scarf, my clothes, my shoes. Their attention makes me slightly uncomfortable, but perhaps it is only appreciation. I suspect I am the first one of my kind to be here in a long while.

The man behind the desk leans forward, resting his chin on his hands. 'Would you like me to conduct your interview in English or Persian?'

English, I respond, feeling mildly relieved.

'But you can speak Persian? We have heard all about it,' he says. I realise now that everything that transpires here is logged and understood.

He asks about my job, my nationality and age. He jots down my replies. He asks why I have come to Iran, and for the names of the places I have been so far.

I have the sense the visa extension form in my hands is worthless. Everything depends on whether they like what they hear.

During the course of our conversation, two or three officials enter without knocking. Each time they see me they stop in their tracks. I can see how high in the ranks I have climbed in the last thirty minutes. These men could ask Hemmatipour to fetch them a cup of tea.

The man behind the desk looks up from his notebook and pauses to study me. 'And how do you meet these women who you say have been teaching you to cook? We cannot be responsible for you if anything happens to you. If you go home, as you say, with strangers you meet in the street.'

I nod to indicate I've understood and he seems satisfied. He asks me a few more questions about my background and I sense that maybe we are nearly done. He turns and translates 'Parents are from Croatia and Hungary' for the other man who until now hasn't spoken, and probably has understood little of what has been said.

He leans back in his chair and slides my passport across the desk towards him. He opens it to my photograph and scans the details, taking note of my date of birth. He checks it quickly against the things he's written down, verifying that I have told him the truth. There is an awkward silence as he studies my photo. He looks at me with what feels like a touch of suspicion.

He asks me to tell him the Iranian recipes I've learned to cook, maybe partly out of interest and partly as a test. Caught off guard, I think first about *tahdig* and *ghormeh sabzi* – but they are recipes that you would find from a cursory glance in any Iranian cookbook. Realising I need to dig deep, I recall something special I'd made with Vahid's mother on our last evening together – *halim e gandom*. It was a stiff purée of boiled wheat, crushed and whipped, fed with a steady trickle of lamb-scented broth. I remember balancing the deep, wide bowl on my forearm while she splashed in half a ladleful of warm yellow broth at a time, while I beat it continually with a fat wooden spoon. The result was a creamy, stringy mass speckled with pieces of onion and lamb, sprinkled with sugar and cinnamon. There was a kind of reverence when we sat to eat it, spooned onto torn pieces of the *sangak* that Vahid fetched especially from the stone bakery, instead of the usual *barbari*. Even Vahid's father paused momentarily to admire it.

He contemplates what I've said and his face appears to lighten. 'You ate this with *sangak* and not *barbari*?'

I nod, assuming it is a trivial question, but he appears to have taken an interest now.

'Yes, it is right. This is the correct way. The sesame on *barbari* would cover the taste.' He says something to his colleague and they nod in agreement. 'It is very good that you have learned to make this recipe yourself. Most women are too lazy to cook this at home any more. If you had time I would invite you to my mother's home to taste her *halim* – her *halim* is famous among all my family.

'You're not planning to get married, are you?' he says suddenly. Again this question. But this time there is nothing accusatory in the way he asks it. Instead there is almost a tone of respect that I choose to be alone. Perhaps he too feels he lives in a place where things not easily understood are quickly dismissed. Perhaps he sees this in me and recognises it for what it is.

Once more he says it, but this time it feels just for show. 'Just so you know, we cannot be responsible if you are taken into a stranger's kitchen and something bad happens to you.'

But we both know a pale girl with talk of butter and rice isn't in any danger. He reaches for the phone.

Chapter Fourteen

Darkness is falling as we return to Kashan. I still feel lost though this is the third evening we have come this way. I can remember the route up to the third turn of the baked-clay walls, past the single shop that stays open late. In its windows are everything one needs for living: packets of still-warm bread, pomegranate jam, the pungent, salty cheese we both prefer. Green bottles of Sehat shampoo, which makes my hair feel like straw and creates suds that never seem to fully rinse.

It has taken us only one full day to shake off our old habit. To stop looking over our shoulders or glancing nervously around. The gentle quiet and absence of nagging questions have given us a fresh start.

I am disoriented by the path to our guest house. The walls, scratched where mopeds have dragged along them, confound me. The white-painted doors held shut with padlocks yield no directional clue. Here and there a pipe or abandoned chair breaks up the symmetry, but otherwise there are no landmarks to guide us.

But Vahid, a child of Yazd's labyrinthine layout, has inbuilt sonar. Though Kashan is new to him too he can navigate it with ease. Eventually we round a corner that I do recognise. Vahid reaches in his pocket for the long, metal key, turning it in the door with some force. The high walls of the courtyard reveal the sky overhead and the faint, distant voices of children mingle with the warm, moist air. Slipping off our shoes and closing the doors to our room behind us, we can shut out what little noise remains. After a relentless tempo of important promises and big things to say, now everything can be spoken in whispers, relaxed and stretched out across several days.

It is here in Kashan I have come to know him. It is here he washes my socks in the basin each evening together with his, draping them over our shoes to dry side by side. I learn that grooming and dressing are collaborative tasks. He leans out of the shower, expecting me to lather soap on his back. He reaches for a comb to pull through my hair. He thinks nothing of asking me to show him my teeth after eating, to flick away a piece of parsley lodged there. He seeks my opinion about which shirt I'd like him to wear that day – though he has only two and both are white.

I learn he likes to change into 'house clothes' as soon as he is settled for the evening, putting on a pair of loose cotton trousers that could pass for pyjamas. By now I know from the tags when he turns them inside out he wears a size thirty-two medium; from the identity cards that spill from the pockets that at nineteen he had a moustache.

I discover that he wore glasses until he had laser eye surgery, just before his father pushed him to join the army. The labels in his clothes are from Iran or Turkey, in an old-fashioned font, bought ready-made from shops in Yazd. He doesn't share the Iranian obsession with designers and brands, the fake logos blaring Gucci and Dolce & Gabbana. I learn that his cousin once went to a party, leaving him at home for refusing to wear such things, a story he tells me one night when we lie in bed, my head resting on his shoulder.

He is superstitious about his health in ways that seem silly, reminding me of my grandmother's old-fashioned beliefs. I laugh sometimes at the expert-sounding tones in his voice, when he counsels or advises me about this or that. If I get a headache he blames it on too much sun. If I have the sniffles it is because we walked facing the wind. He refuses to go out in the mornings with damp hair, believing wet hair is 'like a poison', and insists on blow-drying his hair thoroughly, as well as aiming the hot air for several minutes at each foot in turn. He finds it faintly repulsive when I stir honey into the yoghurt we bring home from the market in plastic bags, sometimes adding mulberries from a tree I find in the road. He believes salty and sweet is a guarantee for a stomach ache, that certain foods were never meant to be combined.

He is willing to make an exception for the way I bake, something he tells me one lazy afternoon. We are side by side on a long wooden bench in the courtyard, sharing a bag of sour green plums sprinkled with salt. 'Let me tell you when I first made something of you,' he whispers, leaning forward so that his breath rustles my hair. 'You were in our kitchen. It must have been your second or third day. And you made that chocolate cake.'

The cake had been my attempt to impress his family. I'd wanted to make something fancy and European. Vahid had been sent to the shops to buy dark chocolate and butter while I'd searched through drawers for something I could use for a whisk. I remember how his parents had reacted, shocked that a cake could require salt and six beaten eggs. That was the first time Vahid had ventured into the kitchen since I'd arrived; normally he avoided it except to wash a plate or grab an orange. He'd stood watching over me, even passing me milk and a spoon. At one point he was so close I could have easily touched him. But my mind was not on such things at that time.

His parents had been aghast at the light, fluffy sponge that had risen, threatening to spill out of the tin. When I served it they ate nothing more than a small, polite mouthful, largely pushing it around on their plates. The next day his mother took to it with a pair of metal spoons, rolling it into dense balls and pressing them into a plate of cheap, puffed-sugar sprinkles. This she passed around and served with tea, pleased to have resurrected my folly.

'Your combination of salt and sugar was new for me,' Vahid remembers. 'You brought something different into our house. I don't know why but I became greedy for your taste. I wanted to hide the cake from everyone else, to eat it all myself and not share it with anyone. It was special, as if baked just for me.'

I feel a surge of warmth listening to him. How he'd come to know me through eating a few simple slices of cake. He'd eaten what no one else had an appetite for, the pinch of salt I considered crucial that had perplexed them at best.

We are the only guests at the house in Kashan, which suits me perfectly. The family are what in Iran would be called 'intellectuals'. The husband, a lawyer, voraciously reads the newspapers in the evenings. His wife studies calligraphy and takes karate lessons. A comfortable ten-year age gap lies between them, a pattern I begin to see is normal between spouses here. I suspect their courtship was at least partly founded in romance rather than the meddling of families, a fact which puts me immediately at ease. They don't ask us a thing about our status, or for the document we have. In fact they couldn't care less about our marriage; they don't ask a thing. I'm awash with gratitude for their indifference, for the fact they appear to take us seriously, though the paper we fought so hard for remains untouched in my bag, which disappoints me a little.

They are warm and welcoming but keep their distance. I suspect they sense our hunger to be be alone together, to cram an entire lifetime into just a few days. We join them for meals but we don't linger. We seek their advice about which traditional houses and gardens to visit, which distilleries of rosewater and marigold have begun harvesting this spring. They give us the name of a driver we call to arrange a trip into the mountains, to see waterfalls and acres of bergamot trees.

Their home, at least four hundred years old, is decorated with rustic style and taste. Its walls are curved and imperfect, its rooms filled with wooden carvings and round silver trays. Their five-year-old daughter leaps between the clay jugs and glazed pots planted with ferns that crowd the courtyard, and tosses scraps of bread to three goldfish circling the square pond in its centre.

In the corner of the garden a clay oven has been recently cast, a deep pit stacked with cherry and olive wood waiting to be set alight. They intend to roast chickens and bake bread in it, they tell us, for the groups they occasionally host from the embassies in Tehran. One of their mothers who also lives with them does most of the cooking, preparing the kind of food that cannot be had easily in restaurants or from stalls in the street. Most foreigners must make do with kebabs, or the strange pizzas twisted into cones and covered with ketchup and mayonnaise, intended primarily for feeding working men and teenagers.

So every few days our routine is broken by a carload of Europeans: the Dutch ambassador's wife or a French trade delegation. The women toss their scarves aside with relief as they enter, admiring the lanterns lit around the courtyard. We are invited to join them, to sit among them on the floor, sharing a vast tablecloth loaded with plates and bowls. We eat hollowed-out quince stuffed with ground lamb and almonds, and hunks of meat with chickpeas and dried limes baked in the oven overnight in stone pots. Vahid, not used to being a paying guest, behaves like a host, showing everyone how to pour the broth into bowls like soup, and mash the meat and chickpeas into a paste. He passes the meat to the foreigners and fills himself instead with the boiled turnips with cinnamon they barely touch.

The whole time I am aware of him, knowing it is his first time mixing with so many outsiders. They talk about places – Bologna, Antwerp, Lyon – he knows only from maps, but has never visited. For once the tables are turned and he is in the minority, not me. Their gaze on us is warm, curious, accepting, lingering only slightly on the ring on my finger but too polite to ask for details. It makes me realise how much I've changed, always preparing to be on the defensive, to having to explain things away.

On the nights when it is just the six of us we eat more simply: a stew with tiny meatballs flavoured with tomato and saffron, roasted aubergines mashed with garlic and turmeric, served with soured cream, that we eat with our hands. The mother makes a special tea from dried quince cores that she urges me to drink. Apparently it is supposed to help me conceive children.

Of course they don't suspect we are using condoms. That we need to be kept separate still. Everything that to them must seem obvious we have ignored or put aside. It makes it easier as I prepare to leave him. Such thinking would only make it worse. I don't know how to describe the feelings I have already, going through the motions of marriage with Vahid in a stranger's house, except that I do so with love. With every new habit I learn or discover it becomes more real, and the more real, the more impossible to imagine that it wasn't always this way.

The room where we sleep is small and plain, not much wider than a metre across. Two cot-like beds are pushed against opposite walls with a narrow length of carpet lying between them. At first we tried to sleep on the floor together, with our bodies half beneath the beds, but I felt pent up and claustrophobic with my head under wood. Instead we spend half the night in separate beds and half together in two-hour intervals. I fall asleep to the sound of Vahid in the bed across from mine, only to wake to find him crushed up beside me, his arms clasped tightly across my shoulders. Normally such a position would make me kick and go crazy but I've come to like the protective nature of the way he holds me, the sense of solidity it brings.

A little mirror hangs just inside the doorway to our

room, a last chance for a quick inspection before stepping outside – to check that a scarf is in a good position, that one's clothes are free of dust and lint. I pause often there and examine myself, looking at my face so that later I'll be able to recall exactly how happy I look.

The days that follow are serene, without confrontation. Seldom, if ever, do we rub up against question or challenge. Like the smoking *esfand* seeds that are whirled around our heads in a glowing tin pan to keep away the 'evil eye' while we sip tea in the bazaar, the paper we hold, though it is never asked for, never demanded, seems to have surrounded us with a protective balm.

When we climb onto buses and Vahid counts his coins to purchase our tickets, people think nothing of tearing two loose from their strips and handing them to us. If my eyes linger for moment on the bread or pastries women are carrying, they insist on passing a generous piece to me to taste. When couples stop us in the street and implore Vahid to make a stern face at their child, a traditional remedy to scare them into behaving for fear of a reprimand from a stranger, he kisses their children's hands, prompting their parents to smile wearily at me, at his kindness in being unable to bring himself to frighten their offspring with even a mock scorn.

We still wake early to go out for soup – a breakfast that has come to mean something more than just food. The cavernous *tabaakhi* have sustained us throughout our courtship, the soup cooks turning a blind eye when we push two chairs into a corner to eat together undisturbed. It is as much from loyalty as hunger that we now seek them out, reaching gratefully, sentimentally, for their plastic seats.

In Kashan the name of the soup changes; the broth is cloudier, swimming with intestines, tripe and the milk teats of sheep. I learn to identify my favourite parts by colour, pointing to the pink spongy membranes that float at the top. With tongs they are lifted from the pot and snipped with a pair of scissors, falling like ribbons into my bowl. Sometimes a sheep's foot, added for gelatine and flavour, is fished out and set on a plate as a gift, which Vahid shreds into our bowls with his fingers. With our soup we eat bread from the *sangak* bakery, which we purchase beforehand, the only point in the day when we are obliged to separate. Vahid stands among the men on the right while I join the women huddled on the left. Orders for stacks of seven or eight *sangak* are called out, folded notes are held in one hand and cotton cloths in another. The wet dough is pulled from buckets or deep steel reservoirs and flattened into ovals, poked with fingers to make small holes. With a flat shovel a man in rubber boots hurls them one by one onto a mountain of pebbles, heated underneath by a roaring gas flame. When each is puffed and crisp it is pulled from the oven and tossed onto a wire-mesh table. In spite of the straight lines I am used to in London, the quiet, firm order to distinguish who is first and who last, there is no confusion here about whose turn it is to grab the next pile of oval loaves, studded with tiny stones.

Vahid carries our rounds of bread over to a row of sharp nails along the wall, impaling them to cool. When they are cool enough to touch, we gingerly pull the hot stones from the dough, letting them drop onto the marble floor. The pebbles are raked up and hurled back into the mouth of the oven, safe from the waiting crowds of black rubber-soled shoes. Vahid folds our bread in half and carries it pressed against his jacket, tearing off the crunchy ends and passing them to me.

We visit the villages where *sharbat* and *golob* are produced, where rose petals, herbs and plants are boiled up and distilled. We have a developed a taste for them, the plastic bottles that are sold in shops everywhere in Kashan – essences of coriander, mint, wild lilac, chestnut blossom. We get through several every day, diluting them with water, adding a spoonful of sugar, sipping them from ceramic mugs. We see the ancient kettles that are set overnight on fires, connected via clear pipes to copper urns. The urns are stood upright in tiny canals dug to channel fresh water from the river to help the vapour condensate and cool. The kettles are opened to show us the mixture inside: halves of oranges, bergamot, a pulp of wild flowers and bark that will eventually be fed to goats. When the urns are uncorked we are urged to lean forward and inhale the scent of the water captured inside, its surface shimmering with droplets of oil.

After our weeks spent in cities, the villages feel friendlier, more welcoming. People come out of their homes but not to question or judge. Gone are the made-up faces, the hairstyles thick with gel, to be replaced with simpler clothes and plainer shoes. The harsh staring and calling out has softened into a gentler concern. It allows us to become tranquil as well, making our way more slowly along the criss-crossing paths.

Vahid asks others to take our pictures as if we are on honeymoon, posing against views of mountains, next to monuments, standing side by side in front of waterfalls. Reviewing some of the photos, I see my hand often clasped around the ring on my finger, twisting it back into place, a gesture that in the course of a few days has already become second nature to me.

One afternoon Vahid took a picture of me without my knowing. I'd been leaning against a brick wall, absorbing the sun's warmth and lost in my own world. Two elderly village women had come out and stood next to me, holding their outer cloaks in gathers around their waists. When Vahid showed me the photo it looked like an organised portrait, the three of us standing side by side. Our eyes were closed and our chins tilted upwards, our elbows jutting out at the same angle. I'd felt inexplicably touched by the details he had captured, the light brown mud on our shoes, the long metal house keys dangling from the women's hands, the quantities of hoses and metal scoops scattered on the pavement. It is one of the few photographs he took of me in Iran in which I look as if I belong, not at all out of place, despite the fact I tower over the other two women by at least a foot.

Only once in all our time in Kashan do I feel us returning to the spotlight we'd been so eager to shun. Vahid is eager to visit a converted *hammam* he'd read about in my guidebook, a spot that is now fashionable for smoking pipes. When we enter through the arch the setting is magnificent. The marble stairwells lead up to unknown passages. The ceiling is a cluster of caps like overturned teacups, thousands of multicoloured glass panels of light. In London such a place would be a museum. But here, where such buildings are in abundance, it has been permitted to decline into a spartan, dimly lit smoking den. Sombre stringed instruments play off a mobile phone hooked up to speakers. Small groups of people huddle in a warren of dark and neglected niches.

We slip off our shoes and step up onto an elevated stone slab beneath a soaring gold and emerald dome. At least forty carpets for sitting on are strewn across the floor. I am barefoot, which I know must be indecent, but in this place it doesn't seem to matter. We choose a spot between two pillars, facing each other. There are scarlet pillows to place behind our backs. I spot two other couples through the dingy lighting, partly hidden by the palms in heavy pots on the floor. They are tucked away in the darkest corners, barely speaking, their voices drowned out by the tinkling fountain in the centre. One girl is wearing a chador at least two sizes two large, the other a black coat and scarf. The boys with them look incongruously stylish with long side-burns and leather jackets, the pockets of their jeans bulging with wallets and packets of cigarettes.

Tea arrives without our asking and Vahid orders a pipe with apple and rose tobacco for us to share. We take turns puffing and blowing smoke, tapping each other on the hand to signal when we are ready to pass the mouthpiece across. I like the serenity that has come lately to Vahid, the settled way he appears in my company. When I glance around me, there is a calm about us, compared with the other couples here.

It is clear there is a plan to it, these girls who blush coyly and sulk, and their male counterparts who act stubborn and deprived. A ritual of tugging back and forth. A pres-sure to give in and deny. A line has been drawn, dictated by the girls, who are forever pushed to go further than they are used to. I wonder how Vahid feels at being spared this experience, at skipping over this chapter of his life. I try to imagine him sitting opposite one of these girls, telling them things they pretend are shocking, watching them clasp hands over their giggling mouths. But I cannot imagine him behaving in such a way.

Sometimes I feel them glance over at us, as if hungry for us to notice their flirting. But Vahid seems to find them tiresome and for the most part looks away. He leans back against the pillar, slipping *salam* biscuits into his mouth, looking pleasantly removed from it all. I know at least half of my appeal must be because I am not from here, because I have allowed Vahid to sidestep the formalities he would otherwise be expected to follow.

I gaze at Vahid and wonder how it can be. Our relationship feels so powerful and sharp. He has readily opened up his life to me, taking pride in sharing with me the things he loves. Our attachment feels bone-deep, irrational, addictive, recalling the kinds of friendships I imagine one has in youth. He took on the mantle of the childhood friend I'd never had, the adult equivalent of the friend who might have woken me on summer holidays by banging on my bedroom window to coax me outside or scratched our names with a twig in the dust.

Many hours he has listened to me as I talked, staring at me or stroking my hair. He is hungry to fill in the most complete picture of every story I tell him. He wants to learn every last detail, asking – when did that happen? Who was that person? His eyes flash with anger and he inhales sharply when I tell him about some difficulty or sadness. He smiles and shakes his head when I describe achievements or triumphs. The pride on his face is fierce and genuine, as if my accomplishments are as much his as my own.

In the one-handed photographs he takes of us standing together, his free hand is always on my shoulder or placed at the back of my neck; sometimes his fingers are clasped gently around my wrist. Always some part of him is attached to my body, seeking contact. The possessive nature of his gestures feels like the purest intimacy.

In relationships I'm used to some barrier or some part being kept off-limits or guarded, but with him I can detect no resistance at all. There are none of the stories men tell women during the first weeks in bed of their past exploits, no quirks or kinky tastes of previous lovers to endure. He has no details for me to confront, no girlfriend to compare me to. With Vahid everything is different. For him there is only me.

Through the pipe smoke there is something perfectly ancient about him, the graceful way he sits, his elbow resting on a scarlet pillow on the ground. It is in these moments I love him most. I feel sorry for the other couples here – for though I know this tug-of-war is probably exciting, it is also sad to be forced into something that must eventually grow tiresome, impossible. Compared with them, with their games and pulling back and forth, I have something direct and real.

The girl in the chador I'd first noticed when we came in repeatedly adjusts and readjusts her cloak, opening her arms wide to spread it out like a cape. She is creating a shield to hide behind, leaning forward each time to be kissed. Moments later another couple disappear into the dark corridor that leads to the toilets. 'Watch,' Vahid says, grinning, 'the owner will have to go after them.' Shortly afterwards they re-emerge, flushed and readjusting their clothes, the proprietor marching them out ahead of him.

He orders them to leave and regards us, sighing loudly, then brings us another pot of tea. 'Come back any time,' he says, paying us a compliment on our good behaviour. 'I am tired of these kids.'

I look across at Vahid, who seems proud, as if perfectly used to being married, responsible, belonging to someone. Once again I'm amazed that he has chosen me, given me a ring, turned away from the pursuit of girls, the rejection, the thrill. It reminds me of those moments when we first knew and disliked each other, when his behaviour had puzzled me and I'd struggled to understand him.

When we leave Kashan I pack our joint possessions in my bag and Vahid assembles a dinner for us to eat on the train.

As I fold up his spare shirt and tuck his wooden comb in among my belongings, I gaze at the ring on my finger. Two more of the diamonds have come loose; soon nearly five of them will have detached and been lost. I have come to know it is a symbol of how everything is fragile – the way some fall freely off, while others cling stubbornly, remaining in place.

We arrive at the station and take our seats in the waiting room, holding tickets purchased from a travel agency the day before. Vahid had confidently spelled out our names, given an assured nod to confirm our intention to sit together. No longer strangers, we get on the train and prepare for the seven-hour overnight journey that will arrive in Yazd at three o'clock in the morning.

His parents had been insistent, calling twice daily, urging us to come back as soon as possible. Occasionally Vahid has passed the phone to me so I could hear their voices, but mostly I relied on him to pass on their wishes. The decision is made without a word. I know he needs me to go there with him. As much as I want to carry on alone with him, I agree to spend my final days with his parents in their home.

Vahid looks happy, even brazen, but I am in a constant state of agitation, not at all sure what to expect. Could I be part of a family without knowing it? Welcomed and accepted, even loved? During the trip I feel reduced to a teenager, hoping for their approval, the agony and anticipation swiping years of stability and confidence to the ground.

The train passes through green, gently sloping countryside, giving way to the mountains of the desert as night falls. Apart from the occasional flickering of lights to indicate a village or town in the distance, we travel in darkness, switching on overhead reading lights to see.

When we pull into the station I get a sense of feverish panic. I want to tell Vahid all the things I've not yet had a chance to say. But there is no time and instantly our four weeks together seem like nothing: a meagre history that could easily be dismantled and put away. Vahid is too eager to see the great strain on my face. I check and recheck myself in the window while Vahid gathers our belongings and guides me to step off the train.

As a daughter, I know how a parent looks at a child who has passed through a milestone or transformation. I've seen the realisation that creeps over their features. I know how these looks are often wet and emotional, how lips can quiver and throats swell. The knowledge is both sweet and painful, like the force of a tide, bringing a child closer before pulling him sharply away. I've learned to recognise it in my own parents on occasions that defined my childhood: when I first walked alone down our kilometre of driveway, clutching my kindergarten lunchbox, or ran the fastest hundred metres in my class at school.

Vahid's father is waiting for us on the platform, wearing a raincoat. On his face there is no trace or acknowledgement of anything momentous. He looks shorter than I remember. He has one hand at his mouth to smother a cough, or maybe a yawn. He searches the crowd for us and Vahid raises his arm to get his attention. When he sees us he walks towards us slowly, his spine rigid. His expression is so aloof and remote that for a second I think about staying on the train. I hang back, feeling a little frightened, now that this moment has arrived.

I stand apart from Vahid on the platform and everything feels like it takes a step backwards. He shakes hands with his father, and I can see him stiffen, his father's arm draped heavily across his back. They become so busily engaged in conversation that I let them go on ahead of me. It feels pointless to walk at their side. I follow behind Vahid, proceeding as if we are strangers. Already he seems many miles away.

Chapter Fifteen

Vahid's mother hugs and kisses him as if he's been gone for months. Then, remembering me standing in the doorway, she steps past him to embrace me. My wedding ring still occupies its place on my left hand; Vahid had insisted I shouldn't remove it.

I recognise at once the familiar scent of their home, the sweet, inky smell of their living room carpet. The foaming lemon soap his mother fills the sink with to wipe the stove. The light is on in the kitchen. The large red pot with one misshapen handle rests overturned in the rack over the sink to dry. The measuring jug for rice is rinsed and hung on a nail, ready for tomorrow.

I get the distinct impression they have accepted what has happened since the last time I saw them. That they understand and have ceded a place in their lives for me. Perhaps Vahid has taken them aside or spoken to them before our arrival or perhaps they sense for themselves something has changed.

Unlike before, I find myself treated with a lack of formality, a clear distinction I am no longer fragile or brittle in their world. Things have become casual. The atmosphere easier. The house is allowed to grow messy and dishes to stay piled in the sink. Tea is no longer arranged on a tray. The single bed in Vahid's sister's room is made up for me, and for the first time I sleep with the absence of company, completely alone.

Normally Vahid's mother would check in on me, be curious to see what I am up to, follow me into the bathroom with a fresh cake of soap. Once, while I am setting out my clothes on the edge of the bed, I catch her staring at me, taking me in. But instead of approaching me as I've come to expect, she retreats, the beaded curtain that separates the bedrooms from the rest of the apartment swinging behind her.

Vahid makes little attempt to hide our closeness. He calls out to me from the shower, to bring him the bottle of shampoo we'd been sharing in Kashan. He spreads blankets on the floor and sprawls out beside me to watch films. I feel embarrassed by him here, squirming when he reaches to kiss my hand when his mother's back is turned. But his parents look unconcerned by his behaviour, and for the most part leave us alone.

Vahid's mother seems quiet, even tired. I sense a growing frustration. When I pour her tea I feel I am not the right person to do it. When we enter the kitchen together to prepare meals, things are quick and perfunctory. Mint is no longer warmed in butter for soup. The final flourish of toasted walnuts and chopped dill is omitted from omelettes. I long for some kind of increased connection, but this too proves impossible. I feel disoriented, even rejected. As if she doesn't want to waste words or prolong our interaction beyond what is necessary.

She too seems at a loss for what to make of me now. One evening she is opening his baby album for me, placing it in my lap and smiling. Inundating me with details, taking me close, pulling me into her world. Then abandoning me. Her moods swing. One moment she is light and calm, the next without humour, dark and pitiless. Sometimes a single act causes her to tilt.

There is a humiliating episode where she goes through all my laundry. I walk into the kitchen to see my dirty underwear scattered across the kitchen floor. She calls Vahid in and asks him to explain to me that she cannot put these items in her washing machine. As I crouch down, I hear her whisper something about it being improper, some medieval notions about my becoming pregnant. I catch a flicker of disgust on her face as I gather my underwear and take it away.

Each time she enters a room I am reminded I do not belong here. I feel overwhelmed by her presence and desperate for air. Anywhere else, I could go out, clear my

head. But I am trapped. Dusty roads of apartment buildings stretch out in every direction. There is no place to go.

The third night I enter my bedroom after brushing my
teeth to find Vahid curled up on the floor next to my bed.
I know such a thing would be shocking to his parents and
nudge him hard with my foot, urging him to wake up, but
he murmurs and pretends to be asleep. I get into bed,
nervous this will be taking things too far. I hold my breath
when I hear his father walk past and brace myself for a
reaction, lying still and partially closing my eyes. Through
the darkness I see his silhouette linger in the doorway. He
pauses, then I hear the creak of the door close and his
footsteps move away.

The next morning there is no mention of it and each
night Vahid continues to roll out his quilt on the floor
next to my bed. If ever there has been a clear signal of
what was going on between us, this must be it. But Vahid's
parents give nothing away. How can they be so capable of
burying their heads in the sand? I wonder. Or is it that
they still view it as some bizarre extension of hospitality,
his sleeping in my room beside me? A big brotherly
gesture, protecting me, the vulnerable foreigner, even
now?

I continue to seek out his mother. I try to fall back into
what I hope is my normal place. In the kitchen I am often
beside her, grinding walnuts and measuring rice, acting
again like the daughter I want to become. One afternoon
I accompany her on a trip to a cemetery, to lay plastic

flowers on the black granite markers of relatives. She clings to my arm for support as her face clouds over and I feel a pleasant sense of being rooted and weighed down. We seem to have achieved an understanding, her affection for me solid and firm.

That afternoon Vahid watches me closely. I understand what it means for him to observe this bond between me and his mother, the peace of mind he craves. Probably it gives him the confidence to do what he does next. He couldn't have imagined the result.

We leave the cemetery to climb into the car. Vahid sits behind the steering wheel. He turns on the ignition and fiddles with the air-conditioning vents, aiming them at where I sit beside his mother in the back.

'I am going to ask my mom if she can imagine you being my wife one day,' he says. He is speaking in English, knowing his mother won't understand.

We smile at each other, hopeful of her approval, and I encourage him with a slight nod. I try to stare out of the car window, pretending I am not aware of what he has planned. Black-clad women clasp the hands of children, making their way through the rows of headstones. Bundles of red and white carnations tumble across the ground in the wind. It makes me feel agitated, wanting the moment to be over with.

He turns around to face his mother and poses his question to her. She shows no reaction and picks at something imaginary in the air. There is such a prolonged silence that

I wonder if she's heard him and I watch Vahid's face crumple with frustration. 'Mama,' he repeats loudly, staring at her.

Then her answer comes, unmistakably firm. It is just a single word: '*Nah.*'

I don't know exactly at what point I start crying as opposed to being on the verge of crying. Weakly, I sink into the upholstery. When we arrive home I collapse in a stunned heap in the courtyard.

The feeling I have isn't of being treated maliciously, or even of being consciously excluded. It is the fact that I am so inconsequential, so clearly beyond the threshold of possibility in their minds. If I have unbalanced things with their plans for Vahid it is only temporary. If I have caused disruption it will all calm down once I am gone. Such is the confidence his parents have in my unsuitability I am not worth considering beyond that.

Affection and sex are out of the question. Or they are sad, desperate acts that feel obscene. Once, we are on the floor of his sister's bedroom after his parents go to sleep, our hands clamped over each other's mouths to muffle the sound. Another we climb into the back of his parents' parked car in the dark basement garage. As we sit in the car afterwards, my underwear around my ankles and the windows fogged up, the wrapper from the condom still in Vahid's hands, I bury my head in my hands and start to cry.

When they are through with me it seems as if I have

never really believed this thing with Vahid would succeed. But in my heart I had kept making myself believe, and even now it is hard not to believe a little. But we will never be any kind of family, and his parents and I will never be close again. From that point things only get worse. I have the clear impression everyone is waiting, fixedly, for me to move on.

Vahid looks as if he's been punched in the stomach. He becomes restless and keeps demanding we go out in the car. 'I don't know what do to,' he says to himself as we hurtle down the highway through the desert at night. In any other situation I'd have been happy beside him, nestled against him as he drives, but on these evenings we feel like refugees.

I glance over at him. But the man who has fought and rallied with such conviction to be at my side has changed into someone lost and defeated. His shoulders are slumped and his face is tense. He has returned to how he looked during the days when I first got to know him, when I found him so bristly and unwelcoming towards me.

Only now do I understand the gravity of what he is up against in trying to go against his parents, how their ideas are shut firmly to anything new. It is heartbreaking that, after a lifetime of living together, they seem to know nothing about what he wants. He isn't inclined towards the heavily made-up cousins with pencilled-in eyebrows whose photographs they have been collecting and placing in front of him for years.

One evening Vahid is so distraught that he pulls the car over and insists we switch places. Behind the wheel I feel instantly more happy and at ease, in control of something for the first time in weeks. Even Vahid seems to relax as we fly along the road as it curves through the mountains, enjoying the sense of open land and sky ahead. We drive in silence and he strokes my hair, kissing me on the cheek as we pass fields dotted with sheep. There is a temporary feeling once again of being free, just the two of us, away from everything that has unhinged us over the past few days.

Vahid instructs me to pull off at an exit and I turn onto a gravelled area of parked cars. Beyond I see a wide, grassy area lit up with fluorescent lights and a large circular fountain. Despite the late hour the park is full of large groups and families, sprawled out on blankets, eating oranges or sunflower seeds spilled out on glass dishes. We walk over to a gentle slope, settling ourselves on two towels Vahid brings from the car. By nature I return to my Yazd mode of behaving, ensuring we sit at least a metre apart.

But Vahid has again used bad judgement. It was the wrong decision to bring us here. We are the only couple present among several hundred families, an anomaly among gatherings between twelve and twenty strong. There are glances of suspicion, even hostility. A punishing tension hangs thick in the air. The explicit message is that we are unwelcome.

In just minutes the police appear. Vahid is again pulled aside and confronted. I listen as they berate him with accusations. 'We had three phone calls from people – asking us to come. This is a place for families. There are children present. You should know better than to be here with a girl alone, especially a foreigner. Where are your parents anyway?'

Once more Vahid empties his pockets of army paper-work and laminated ID cards. Once again he is reduced to a small rubble of dates for the officers to rake through. The same disproportionate response – sitting on a grassy hill earns us a visit from not one but three police officers. The eating has stopped and chins gesture in our direction. My limbs begin to shake. I am tired of feeling singled out and humiliated. It aggravates the growing sense of failure I have, to be always on the wrong side of rules that must not be broken and expectations that must be met.

During our time in Kashan I had occasionally allowed myself to imagine we might one day travel together. I wanted him to see my favourite cities and discover new places. I pictured us cycling along canals, buying felafel and carrot juice from the Turkish market in Berlin, or pluck-ing bitter oranges from trees and eating chestnuts from street carts in Jerez. I thought the jumbled, mishmash cul-ture of European cities would suit him, make it easier for him to get used to life outside of Iran. Later when he'd adjusted we'd go further and further, riding dilapidated ferries to islands in Asia, hitching lifts to near-empty beaches in Brazil. I didn't even know whether he knew how to swim.

The idea had crossed my mind, even, of having a child one day together. I'd seen a boy once when we were wandering in the old section of Yazd who could easily have been our son. We'd been searching for a herbalist Vahid knew about. Maybe I'd already been in a fanciful mood. A man we'd passed on the way and asked for directions had smiled and warned us to be careful, saying the shop sold things possessing magical powers. When we found it, it felt more like a cave, deep and dark and cold enough to make me shiver. The walls were lined with sheets of aluminium foil and the shelves creaked under countless jars of herbs and powders. Only two people could enter at a time for there was little space to stand among the great sacks of dried flowers and leaves piled on the floor.

As we squeezed inside, Haji Akbar – the herbalist – came to me and stared me down. His expression was so severe it made me jump. His burly white eyebrows shot up at such sharp angles I'd been at a total loss for what to say. In retrospect I imagine he'd meant to show concern, assuming we'd come a long way to seek him out. I wish I had thought of going with a list of ailments needing curing, or some mysterious ache or illness only he could relieve. Instead I'd pointed around his shop, trying to recover my nerve, directing him to this or that and reaching for my money. We'd emerged with a jar of murky honey for me to take home and a small plastic bag of white *golpar* seeds to eat with boiled green beans.

When my eyes readjusted to the daylight outside I saw the boy. His skin was smooth and he had fierce green eyes. I stopped and stared at his sandy hair and olive skin. He kicked up the dust by scuffing his shoes along as he walked, seeming to enjoy the little clouds that puffed up in his wake. With his colouring and the odd, independent way he had about him he could easily have been ours, mine and Vahid's. Instead of giggling or shouting 'Hello' he simply gazed back at me. There was no menace or fear in his expression, just the impression of unflinching boyishness and being secure on his own turf.

When he'd passed I suggested the idea to Vahid, that if we were ever to have a child together it would resemble that boy. Vahid had laughed and insisted that our child would be even more handsome, as if there was nothing more that needed to be said.

When the police are finished with us we go home. I feel certain there can't be anything else. When we step out of the car the security guard calls Vahid over. I am left to stand alone in the street. I watch them speaking, looking for some clue in their expressions.

'Jenny, the police were here yesterday,' Vahid tells me, motioning me over. 'They followed us here the day we came home from the train station. They saw you and thought you might be a spy so they came yesterday to make trouble for us.'

The guard tells us they had demanded to know where I was staying. When he'd refused they had pushed him and shouted, insisting he write down a list of everyone in the building, their apartment numbers and all of their names. I watch his face as he retells the events and recounts his refusal; I see his pride in having protected us. My presence seems to have given him a sense of purpose, a catalyst to rise up against the *basiji*.

Though I am aware it is a serious matter, it is also absurd. I try to imagine men in uniforms pounding on the door of Vahid's apartment and rifling through my notes and photographs – revealing only recipes and pictures of food. Vahid looks strained as he leads me away. The message is clear to us both. It appears everyone is waiting for me to leave.

So we depart first thing the next morning, taking a taxi to the train station instead of anyone driving us. We leave in total darkness like criminals; everything has been packed in haste. We half haul, half drag our bags along, our belongings shoved haphazardly into pockets and unzipped pouches. We shiver as we stand together on the platform, waiting for the train bound for Tehran. Sadly it feels like the perfect way to depart. In fact, it is the only way.

Chapter Sixteen

This isn't where I had expected us to spend our last night together, in a place so far outside of Tehran. In the distance there is only a motorway and endless, scarred earth where identical apartment complexes are being planned and built.

Everything here has a half-finished look to it. Some of the mounds of soil have been there long enough to sprout yellow wild flowers. Others have developed a crust firm enough to sit on. Some enterprising person has taken advantage of all the fresh dirt and started growing a small patch of vegetables. Neat rows of tomato and aubergine plants have begun to fruit. A carefully engineered canopy of sticks and torn strips of plastic sheets has scared the birds away long enough to give it a chance to thrive. In this landscape of torn-up ground, barren buildings and wind-blown garbage, it gives the impression of being the sole thing that has received any care.

The apartment where we will sleep is in between tenants. The previous inhabitants moved out a week ago, leaving traces of their residency in the form of an abandoned sponge on the edge of the sink and a lining of soiled aluminium foil under the burners of the stove. Decorated in mustard and green, the apartment looks intended for middle-class families. A low sectional couch is arranged in front of a picture window covered with thick blue curtains. The bathroom has a European-style toilet instead of a squat hole in the floor. Shared taxis stop just at the top of the hill, ferrying people onwards to central Tehran neighbourhoods like Shemroon and Tajrish, or beyond to the industrial city of Karaj. It is a commuter suburb much like those in other cities. The shop downstairs sells bread and tiny, finger-length cucumbers, which together with some cheese, mint and olives will form our last meal together.

The apartment belongs to Vahid's old commander in the army – it had taken Vahid over twenty text messages and a network of phone calls to obtain the keys. As we'd sat on the train, Vahid had begun calling everyone he knew in Tehran with any kind of power, working his way through the phone numbers of those he'd served with in the army. Everyone he talked to seemed to take an interest. Word spread like wildfire that he had entered some kind of marriage. There seemed to be an unspoken understanding that he needed somewhere safe to pass a night with his new wife.

We'd had hours to kill until we could get the keys. In Tehran we had passed the time moving from place to place. The rain had prevented us from staying anywhere long. We'd sat in the steamed-up windows of a cheap café, spending the last of our money, ordering lamb's brain sandwiches, fried on a griddle and stuffed into split rolls with ketchup. Football commentary had played on the radio. The young guys who manned the kitchen took turns slipping outside for a cigarette. I'd felt a powerful sense of guilt towards Vahid for what I was about to do, for effectively abandoning him.

When we arrived in Tehran I could see Vahid was a bit clueless. Aside from his military posting he'd had little opportunity to learn the city. He knew as much as I did, that wealth was north and poverty was south, and aside from that we were lost.

As we walked around, it was like any other Iranian city we'd known, compartmentalised into neighbourhoods devoted to various trades. Kalhor Street was an endless row of shops selling automotive parts. Manoochehri Street sold Caspian Sea sturgeon and river trout from large tanks. The vegetable shops clustered around Engelhab Square sold things like avocados and rosemary, items I hadn't seen for weeks. Probably the biggest difference was how little anyone bothered us – no one looked at us at all. In the rush of people who could have been in London or New

York if it weren't for the Farsi signs and the boxy shape of the cars, we had all but disappeared.

The anonymity had lessened our anxiety. Though we were tired and our eyes were heavy we were happy to be away together again. We walked through an Azeri neighbourhood of southern Tehran, slipping into the courtyards of old 1920s mansions overgrown with vines and rose bushes. We sucked on small squares of jelly and candied walnuts, and kissed when no one was around. We shared a kind of desperation, making a last attempt to forge our relationship into something solid. We wandered the streets, waiting until we could go to the place where we would spend the night.

We passed a small mosque that made me stop. I heard the desperate sounds of crying from within. A plaque above the door read 'God curse the killer of Fatemeh'. 'Noor Mosque' was spray-painted in green letters below.

Two men approached, extending their arms and seeming eager for us to go inside. Over my shoulder I heard one of them whisper to Vahid, asking if I wouldn't be afraid. The building appeared modest, even shabby, nothing like the grand mosques I'd grown accustomed to entering, decorated in seven soaring shades of turquoise and emerald. It lacked their immense pillars and vast, domed arches, their intricate façades that had taken fifteen years to build. Instead it was plain, covered in chalky, white stucco. The entrance was strung with wires and lit by a single, round light.

In stark contrast to the miserable wailing and sobbing inside, the heavy, wooden doors were painted a vibrant green. Tentatively I reached to open one, pushing it carefully but firmly with my palm.

The noise was shrill and powerful, the moaning and crying out rang in my ears. I turned to leave, unable to bear it, but Vahid grabbed my arm, steadying me. My eyes began to adjust to the darkness. Faintly I could make out a sloped aisle and a wooden bench. Guided by my hands, I stumbled quickly to take a seat, terrified we'd trespassed on a funeral of some kind. I strained my eyes to anticipate any movement, half expecting someone to come and ask us to leave. The room was pitch black, the darkness absolute. I couldn't even see the shoes on my feet.

I heard shrieks of people's names. Moans for help and forgiveness. Pitched voices of sickening wretchedness. I lowered my head even though no one could see me, my cheeks burning with confusion and guilt.

I felt Vahid slide across next to me. He leaned over and pulled my scarf away from my ear. Careful to make himself heard, he explained we had entered a mourning mosque, a special gathering place for those racked by sorrow and grief. The windows had been blacked out to conceal identities. The lights were switched off to protect the proud or the shy. We squinted in the darkness, inhaling the smell of old carpets, the bones in our chests vibrating.

It seemed to me incredible that Iranians, in spite of their carefully nurtured privacy, in spite of not even calling each other by their names in public, should be so forthcoming with the most personal expressions of mourning, preferring to gasp and howl them in the darkness of this room. My fear slowly changed to a feeling of calm, even liberation, the freedom of being able to weep openly without shame. Vahid placed his hand lightly over mine and it felt right to be there together, in that pitch-black, morose, intimate place.

I wish the thought hadn't come, but it rose up and took hold before I could push it away. I knew it was time now to give him up, for Vahid to become a stranger again. His life would continue to be shaped by people and events that were nothing to do with me.

I thought of him alone in the coming months, returning to everything he knew. Sheltering again among his family, looking for a job, perhaps finding himself forced to grow a beard. He had no passport, had never left the country. And anyway, since he was Iranian, where was there for him to go?

Now as I look at Vahid in the shabby apartment he seems apologetic. It isn't where I had expected us to spend our last night together. I don't know what I expected at all. A feast prepared in his mother's kitchen? Dozens of exulting relatives seated all together on the floor?

I can see the shame in his eyes for having brought me here. But I know it is the best he can do for me and I try to assure him that it is fine. My bag is on the mat by the door; there had been no point in unpacking it. There is no bed so we'll sleep on top of blankets piled on the carpet. A small heater is plugged into the wall beside us. A plastic sheet with our simple dinner is laid out on the floor.

Lying together on our nest of sheets and covers, Vahid tells me I need to come back to him. His eyes fill with tears and his voice becomes hoarse. I can hardly bear to look at him. I know that as much as he might make me happy he would also make me miserable. I don't know whether we would even survive together or what we would be up against. Maybe in Tehran we could make some kind of existence for ourselves. Or maybe he could try to come to the UK, causing the tables to turn. I would be forced to become his mentor and parent, to guide and sustain him in finding a new life. Everyone there would believe he was lucky to come, seeing it as an escape from some kind of nightmarish, wasted land. Only I would understand how he would suffer and long for all he would be leaving behind.

There is little left for us now. A final, tender, excruciating sex and a few hours of restless sleep before the taxi comes for us at 4 a.m. Forty-five minutes in the taxi, five minutes to push my luggage through the chaotic security barricades, another ten to find the sign bearing 'London' in rearranged letters. Maybe we'll be left with twenty minutes to sit in some quiet place under the gaze of the men at the exit control who will check my passport and visa and scratch at it with their fingernails. Then I'll pass through, unaccompanied by Vahid for the first time in weeks, and disappear.

Eleven Memories
I am Taking with Me

nimeh ye zohr – the position of the sun in the sky when it produces no shadow on the ground, our least favourite time of day.

taarof – the number of times a gift must be refused before it can be accepted, to allow a person without means to show generosity without hardship.

jigar – the liver, the organ said to feel emotion, like the heart, but because the liver is composed only of soft tissue, it is said to be the most vulnerable.

noon khoshk – the scraps of bread Vahid's mother collected in a bag on the back of the kitchen door, to be handed to a man who came to their neighbourhood twice a week and sold the bread on for feeding animals.

livaan – the metal cup Vahid carried with him everywhere, filling it with water at fountains so we could drink from it.

tokhmeh khordan – the way Vahid taught me to eat sunflower seeds, breaking the shell between my teeth and sucking out the seed in a single motion, getting only a faint taste of salt from the shells.

yaaftan – to find something beautiful in a place where it is least expected or where you had to struggle.

payvand zadan – the act of locking two things to each other to keep them both safe, an old-fashioned word for marriage.

joob – the canals running down the sides of the streets in Yazd, carrying water from wells to the pomegranate and cypress trees.

gholob gholob – the sound Vahid made when drinking the warm milk and orchid root his mother made for him as a child.

roon e morgh – the leg of a chicken, Vahid's favourite part, which he stripped of meat with his teeth before sucking on the bone. Also a name he gave to me.

Chapter Seventeen

Opposite us a woman is reading a book and taking bites from a sandwich wrapped in foil. Two girls are staring into their compacts and relining their eyes with pencils. A man repeatedly stands up and reaches into his pockets, then sits again, counting the passports of himself, his wife and three children. Five minutes pass. Then ten. I watch the letters on the departure board spin and arrange themselves into new destinations, then people slowly get up and walk away.

The barrier they must pass through has a finality about it – two counters where a last inspection takes place. I've heard that people have been stopped here just before leaving the country, had passports confiscated, been taken to prison. Today everyone passes through without incident. Soon it is just the two of us left.

We are too numb even to drink from the paper cups of tea in our hands, yet too alert to be able to relax. Here we must be more careful than anywhere, to ensure the guards don't see anything amiss. Every few minutes their eyes pass over us with little interest, like some tiny nothing. Only this is the opposite of nothing.

It is something that began with a simple hello in a garden, an address scribbled into a notebook, an invitation to learn to cook rice with a crust. In four and a half weeks it has both betrayed and refused to abandon me, clearing all other men away. It is something that causes me now to sit, twisting a still-strange-feeling ring on my finger, staring at the floor in shock.

I shut my eyes hard to trap the tears behind my eyelids, to force them to be reabsorbed before they have the chance to spill down my face. I feel the corners of my lips begin to give way and tremble. I am the one leaving, the one with a paper ticket in my hand, but it feels as if it's the other way around – that Vahid is being torn away from me.

I am familiar with the course our relationship should now take. The emails, the expensive phone calls, the slow, inevitable eroding that will follow; the strange logic that submerges us into the lives of others and then, just as forcefully, rips us away. I'm fearful of the things that will no longer make sense when I am home, or that the whole time I will just be thinking of him.

I glance again at the departure board, where the green light next to 'London' has begun to flash, then at the destinations below waiting to be lit up. I don't know what I am hoping for. Aside from a handful of European capitals, it reveals only a list of large, soulless cities across the Middle East: Doha, Abu Dhabi and Dubai. I feel desperate and disappointed. But then I look again. And I see it.

I turn to Vahid and he looks at me. I study his face and try to think how to ask. My cheeks are hot and I press on them with my hands.

'Meet me in Istanbul,' I say. 'In two and a half months' time. I have a friend who has an apartment. We can borrow the keys. You have time to get a passport and you won't need a visa for Turkey. I'll have a break between classes for the summer. We can be . . . I pause and my voice catches in my throat. 'We can be together again.'

He looks tired and his eyes fill with tears. Without saying a word I see inside him and pull out his answer. I recognise the same hunger and courage in his expression, the same glow of tenderness and hope. I feel a tidal rush of emotion and gratitude. A new road is available to us.

I reach for my bag. Vahid places his hand on mine. Then, his back is to me, leaving me to walk forward and wipe the tears falling down my face.

The guard stares at me and I compose myself. I feel the weight of each gesture, the stamp he places in my passport, the tearing of my boarding pass, all dragging me away.

I stop to look behind me one last time for Vahid but he is gone, probably already fighting his way into a shared taxi. Back again to his old ways of travelling. Anonymous and nimble once more without me.

As I move forward, my sadness gives way to something bigger, an urgency and a willingness to open up my life and come to him again. In some small way this rash agreement has given us a kind of power, one we've forfeited up until now.

Epilogue

I returned to Iran two more times in the following year. Vahid moved to Tehran where he'd found a job, and we lived there together for short periods in a small apartment.

During that time Ahmadinejad was re-elected. Two million people took to the streets. News channels around the world replayed footage of Neda collapsing to the pavement, blood spilling out of her nose and mouth. There were rallies, anti-Western demonstrations. Embassies and foreign companies were shut down.

In between those visits we met everywhere we could. Tbilisi. Yerevan. Twice in Istanbul. Anywhere Vahid's Iranian passport could take him.

Then, one cloudy Thursday evening, just over a year after we'd first met, I went to Heathrow to pick him up and bring him home.

On the way to the airport I had tried to imagine him leaving Iran: closing the door to the apartment we'd shared together, taking a taxi alone to the airport because no relatives would drive him, and staring out of the airplane window at the hazy, fading skyline of Tehran. I imagined the courage and leap of faith that it had taken for him to come here, to London, to me.

When Vahid broke the news to his parents that he was leaving, his mother had said, 'Jennifer's blade is sharper than ours.'

The everyday certainties of my city are all mysteries to him and I feel a proud, protective joy in watching him discover and decipher them one by one. I catch his musky scent when we sit together in the stoic silence of the British Library. I smile as he laps at salted caramel ice-cream cones and dunks the base into a cup of sweet, black tea. I love that he still shakes my hand when we meet in public, but now accompanies his greeting with a wet kiss on my cheek. On our fingers we wear new, simple silver bands, the result of a quiet ceremony at a register office, held on a Tuesday afternoon.

It's hard to imagine an Iran where we could walk so freely, go unquestioned, or be permitted a three-dimensional life. Iran, for all its magic, has pushed us into exile. We don't talk about it but I know we are both nervous, even fearful, about whatever future lies ahead for us. Our relationship has been stitched together out of fragments of devotion, strong will and despair, and made us sometimes restless and brittle. But the arc of our history is a wonder to us; the powerful trajectory that has brought us to this place regularly makes us stop: to smile, to reach across the table to one another and to shake our heads in unison at the journey we have taken so far.

virago

To buy any of our books and to find out more about Virago Press and Virago Modern Classics, our authors and titles, as well as events and book club forum, visit our websites

www.virago.co.uk
www.littlebrown.co.uk

and follow us on Twitter

@ViragoBooks

To order any Virago titles p & p free in the UK, please contact our mail order supplier on:

+ 44 (0)1832 737525

Customers not based in the UK should contact the same number for appropriate postage and packing costs.